MORE GHOSTS OF THE ISLE OF WIGHT

BY

GAY BALDWIN

Gay Baldwin.

MORE GHOSTS
OF THE
ISLE OF WIGHT

BY

GAY BALDWIN

FIRST EDITION

NOVEMBER 1992

The first ever collection of local ghost stories "Ghosts of the Isle of Wight" written fifteen years ago with Ray Anker, has been a local "best seller" since the first edition sold out in just three weeks.

Now Island journalist Gay Baldwin has written another book on the supernatural and a third is in preparation. Almost everyone enjoys a good ghost story and this new collection of 75 haunting tales from all over the Island should send a shiver down the spine.

Although not a "proper" Islander, Gay has lived on the Island since the age of four, and was educated at Whippingham Primary and Carisbrooke Grammar Schools.

Her career as a local journalist has spanned more than 20 years, much of this spent as a news reporter and feature writer with the IW County Press.

She lives at Cowes, with husband David, daughter Victoria, and a collection of Siamese cats.

I.S.B.N 0-9520062-0-0

Printed by Crossprint Ltd., Daish Way, Dodnor, Newport, IW.
Published by Gay Baldwin, 9 Pine Tree Close, Cowes, IW.
(0983) 294651

Cover design and frontispiece by Mei Trow.

Photographs by Mike Mackrill.

CONTENTS

WHO BELIEVES IN GHOSTS?

A Ghost Hunter's Guide

According to the dictionary a ghost is:- a spirit appearing after death, the soul of a man, a phantom, apparition, spectre, spook, visitant, revenant and wraith.

When I decided to write this follow-up to "Ghosts of the Isle of Wight" I was concerned that it might be difficult to find enough stories to make the project worthwhile. I needn't have worried. Accounts of new hauntings came flooding in. At one stage I began to think it was remarkable to find a house without a ghost of some sort.

In the fifteen years since the first book was published, attitudes to ghosts and the supernatural have undergone a considerable change. People of all ages are interested in the subject and willing to keep an open mind on something they don't understand.

Ghosts can, and do, appear almost anywhere. A house needn't be old or historic to have one. Some very interesting hauntings have been reported in a new housing estate in Wootton and in council offices in Newport. Mischievous poltergeists play tricks on the unwary in shops and cafes. Ghostly soldiers haunt some of the Island's Victorian forts, while out at sea and on lonely beaches, phantom ships still sail and ghosts of smugglers walk.

Some apparitions appear at set times each year, like the long-vanished manor house of Knighton Gorges, which is said to materialise on New Year's Eve; other ghosts come and go at random, sometimes with years between sightings.

A few hauntings consist of nothing more than a sound; the tread of footsteps; ghostly music; the rustle of silk or sharp knocking noises - the traditional 'things that go bump in the night'.

Some ghosts talk, whisper, shout and argue, seeming aware of their surroundings, while others are oblivious to everything, following centuries-old pathways through walls, walking above or below present-day ground and floor levels.

Many families who live in a haunted house love the warm friendly atmosphere that their ghost engenders. They like having it around, often talking to it, giving it a name and treating it like a family pet. Occasionally it really is, for in some homes the ghost of a favourite animal lingers on.

Who can see ghosts? Almost anyone it seems. Even confirmed sceptics have had their minds changed after witnessing the evidence with their own eyes. People of all ages see, hear and smell ghosts. Reliable, intelligent, credible professional people have come forward with their stories. Many of them are puzzled and continue to be haunted by what they have seen and experienced. A few have turned to the Church for help and exorcisms have been performed with varying degrees of success.

Ghosts themselves come in all shapes and sizes. Some appear solid and real while others are wispy and ethereal. They have been described as a reflection in a plate glass window; while others are made up of dots or sparks of energy. In a few instances only part of the ghost has materialised, a disembodied hand or foot, head or torso.

In collecting these accounts I have looked at the history behind a haunting. In many cases there is an obvious explanation; someone has been murdered, committed suicide or died a sudden and often violent death. Does tragedy, unhappiness or despair leave its imprint on place? Can emotion linger in the atmosphere or in the fabric of a building like a psychic recording, to be replayed at intervals when the right atmosphere or someone who is receptive and on the same wavelength comes along?

In other cases I can find no apparent reason for a ghost's appearance. The spirit just doesn't want to move on. It is content to remain in its former home. The haunting is inexplicable.

I would like to thank everybody who has helped with my researches and those who have welcomed me into their homes and agreed to their names, addresses and stories being used. It cannot be easy to tell a complete stranger that you have a ghost. Special thanks to Mike Mackrill for the photos, Mei Trow for the cover and frontispiece designs, Ray Anker for his help and advice and to my long-suffering family who are now used to me calling out, "That one's got a ghost," whenever we go for a drive and spot a house I have visited.

I, incidentally, have never encountered a ghost, although I have been around many haunted houses. When asked if I believe in ghosts I reply, "Yes, ghosts do exist, but I don't know what they are, why they appear, or why certain people see them and others don't. I have a feeling that some time in the future an explanation will be found." Until then I shall continue to collect stories. I am already working on a third book of Isle of Wight ghost stories and would welcome your contributions. I must apologise to anybody who can't find their story in this book. I simply ran out of space and have had to hold several chapters back for the next volume.

There are stories here to make you both shiver and smile. Laugh if you wish. I agree there's nothing quite so funny as the idea of a ghost......until you happen to meet one.

CHAPTER ONE

GHOSTLY NEWPORT

A DARK AND VIOLENT TRAGEDY

A bloodstained nightgown and a little leather shoe are the only evidence of a dark and violent tragedy that ended in a double murder more than two centuries ago. The scene of the crimes was the old Sun Inn at Holyrood Street, Newport, where for over two hundred years one of the innocent young victims has waited to tell her poignant story.

Half-forgotten rumours of the murders are still told by old Newport folk, but it was not until Graham Morris bought the former coaching inn after it closed in 1976, that he made a gruesome discovery in a tiny hidden attic room.

Graham, who now runs a shop dealing in antique militaria in part of the building, was renovating the old pub with his partner, builder Dave Knight, when he discovered the room which had been boarded up and wallpapered over many years before. It had clearly lain empty and undisturbed for a very long time for all it contained was a soldier's pillbox hat.

However, hidden in a void behind the chimney he came upon a dusty bundle of rags and a bag of ancient leather shoes. Inside the bundle was a very old white cotton nightgown decorated with broderie anglais.....and heavily bloodstained. "It was covered in congealed blood which had gone brown with age and was absolutely macabre. It made me feel very uneasy. I burnt it in the back yard," Graham confessed.

In that same yard, he and Dave discovered an old well which also played a part in the tragedy. It contained at least 33 feet of water and although the well was pumped out by the IW Fire and Rescue Service, it was never explored or excavated because the firemen deemed it too dangerous. The well has since been filled in.

The old pub was originally built in 1640 as a gentleman's residence. When it became a coaching inn is not clear, but it was certainly in use as early as 1730 as a busy staging post, with stabling in the nearby yard of what became Read's Posting Establishment.

The Victim Tells Her Tale

Among the old shoes found by Graham was a small leather ankle boot, which was shown to a local nurse, Mrs Ivy Griffith, who has been a medium for many years. Ivy would often sit holding the little shoe to try to pick up some feelings from it.

Over the following year, she and another medium were able to piece together the story of those tragic events at the Sun Inn, as fragments of information were relayed to them by the spirit of a young French girl named Francesca, who had once owned the shoe and nightgown.

"One day a very insistent little voice came through, asking 'Parlez-vous Francais?' Every time we had a sitting, she was there again. She told us her name was Francesca and that she was thirteen years old."

Once the Sun Inn at Newport. This old building harboured a gruesome and bloody secret.

Did Francesca once wear this little leather shoe?

Bit by bit the girl's pathetic story came out. It seemed she had been bought by the landlord of the inn for three crowns and put to work as a skivvy and serving wench. An orphan born in France, she spoke little English and was very unhappy. A tiny slip of a girl, she had long curly fair hair and large dark-lashed eyes.

Francesca had been kept busy running to and fro with tankards of ale until late into the night. She told Ivy how the customers would cheer the dog fighting and cock fighting that went on in the pub, while she watched the excitement through a crack in the rafters of her attic room.

Francesca fell in love with Ralph, a young stable lad at the Sun Inn which was the staging post for coaches running between Cowes and Ryde. Ralph was kind to her and she started to blossom. Unfortunately the little serving wench also caught the attention of the owner of a local print works, a man of standing and a pillar of the community. He watched and waited his chance. One night he found her alone in the attic....

Francesca became pregnant, but she did not understand what was happening to her body until she felt the child within her quicken. She went into premature labour and, haemorrhaging on her white cotton nightgown, she lay close to death.

Francesca gasped out the name of the father and how he had had his way with her. To prevent a scandal which would have ruined him in the town, a few of his friends strangled the little French girl and dumped her body in the well. To cover the killers' tracks and shift the blame, a scapegoat was found. Young Ralph was named as her lover and murderer. He, too, had to die.

Late one night, led by a local one-eyed ruffian known as the 'Pigman', a drunken rabble threw a rope over one of the old beams, stood the struggling boy on a crate, and then kicked it from under him. They left his body hanging there all night while they drank and caroused around it. Next morning he was cut down. His corpse followed Francesca's into the well.

"Once she had told us the whole story, we never heard from Francesca again. She had wanted to have her case heard, as she put it, and for Ralph's name to be cleared. It took many months to piece all this together. You can't rush spirits," Ivy said knowingly.

Francesca and Ralph are together now, and have been for two centuries. "We are very happy now," she told Ivy. Apparently her only regret is that she was not able to watch her child growing up.

Ivy still has that little shoe, but any aura of sadness has been dispelled, purged and cleansed by Francesca herself.

Never Mock a Ghost

In the flats above the two little shops, however, things have not been quite so peaceful. Some years ago a poltergeist terrified two families there (a detailed account of this haunting is given in Ghosts of the Isle of Wight).

Recently, Dave Knight, his wife Glenda and some friends were having a drink in one of the flats where their son and his girlfriend were living. Glenda told them the tale of the bloodstained nightgown. Everyone just laughed.

Suddenly a picture jumped off the wall and fell to the floor right across the room. The string wasn't broken, and no-one had been near it when it fell. The room went very quiet. Suddenly Francesca's story did not seem so far-fetched after all......

"Ghosts do not like to be mocked," warned Glenda.

THE PHANTOM KING

As one of Newport's oldest and most historic buildings, it is only fitting that the King James I Grammar School, which since 1618 has stood at the corner of Lower St James' Street and Lugley Street, should be haunted.

King Charles I stayed there for sixty days in 1648, prior to signing the Treaty of Newport, using the large oak panelled schoolroom as his presence chamber and sleeping in the room directly above. It was there, at dawn on November 30, that the king was seized by the Army and taken to Whitehall for his trial and subsequent execution.

In the centuries since, the school prospered, and many generations of Islanders were taught within its venerable old stone walls. It ceased to be a school in 1963, but five years later youngsters' voices rang out once more when it became a youth centre. Youth leader Graham Dove knows the old school has its ghosts. He has both heard and felt them.

Supernatural activity seems to be centred around the first floor room above the headmaster's office, the one in which the unfortunate king slept.

Footsteps are heard when the building is empty, echoing through deserted rooms. One youth leader who spent a night in that bedroom wouldn't go back again. Although it had been midsummer, he said the room had gone icy cold and he had felt very clammy and uncomfortable.

As youth centre members are intrigued by tales of ghouls and ghosts, Graham and the other leaders often organise "Fright Nights" in the old school which are immensely scary - and popular.

It was when they were clearing up after one such night in that bedroom that they, too, noticed a sudden drop in temperature. Something unseen walked through the room and out of the door."We all felt it. There was something in there with us. The footsteps went right across the room and out onto the landing," Graham said. Whatever walks there enjoys company, for last winter, when the building was closed and locked, figures could be seen moving around a room lit by dim and flickering candles. It was that first floor bedroom again, of course.

One of the old school's ghosts has actually been captured on film. A photograph of Colin McMaster of Newport, taking part in karate championships held in the school grounds, shows a figure in a Cavalier's costume standing at the window behind.

"I thought someone was having us on when I first saw these," Graham frowned. But then he realised that the window had been blocked by heavy weight training equipment. No-one mortal could have been looking out of that room where King Charles spent his last days.

A ghost captured on camera appears in this photograph of a karate demonstration at the old King James Grammar School, Newport. The faint figure is visible in a boarded-up window next to the room in which King Charles I spent two months.

The Mauve Lady

Graham is certain that another of the school's ghosts is a woman. It is her footsteps he hears when the building is empty, and she has also been seen walking up and down Lugley Street. Affectionately known as the Mauve Lady of Lugley Street because of the mauve crinoline dress she wears, this gentle ghost haunts solicitors' offices there.

In 1979 she was seen by two visiting Americans who were sheltering from a sudden thunderstorm in the doorway of Lamport Heyes and Co, next door to the old school. They saw a figure in a long cloak cross the road towards them and, commenting on the downpour, said, "What awful weather this is."

The woman said "Aye" in apparent agreement and walked past them....straight through the solid wooden door.

Staff at the solicitors' office have not yet seen her, but have occasionally heard her footsteps tap-tapping up the stairs, and have searched for her in vain. "We are quite used to it by now," said secretary, Margaret Snow.

Meanwhile, back at the youth centre, caretaker Ray Edwards and his wife Joan, have become accustomed to the sweet smell of hay wafting down the staircase late at night after the youngsters have gone home.

In the building now used as offices, the school's horses were once stabled. The lofts overhead are storerooms; not a wisp of hay has lain there for many years. But, on a warm, still evening, the old sweet aroma fills the air and sometimes riding boots are heard mounting those stairs....

GHOST WITH A SENSE OF FUN

Ghostly goings on in a council office hit the headlines when women working in South Wight Borough Council's old offices in Newport were so scared that they called in the police.

While working overtime on the new electoral register, the six women all heard heavy footsteps in an empty office overhead; the sound of a chair being dragged across the floor; and a door opening. Mrs Margaret Chandler who now works at the council's Sandown offices, said they had all been petrified.

"The policeman made a thorough search but didn't find anything. After he had gone the noises started again, but we decided to stick it out. After that, we got quite used to strange things happening, and nicknamed our ghost 'Fred'.

"We never saw him but I am convinced there is a ghost in the old building. He would sometimes take things such as scissors, pencils and other small objects, but would always bring them back again later. I am sure he had quite a sense of humour."

Heavy doors with spring closers would fly open, cupboard doors would also be opened and footsteps would be heard in empty corridors. The offices in Pyle Street incorporate Chantry House, originally one of Newport's religious foundations dating back to 1449. The present house was built in the mid 1720s.

Margaret worked at the Pyle Street offices, formerly the old Rural

District Council offices from 1966 until they closed in 1990. "I said when we moved out that poor old Fred would be lonely," she added.

Margaret was often teased by colleagues who didn't believe in ghosts. However, she had the last laugh when a local postman confirmed her story. His mum had worked as cleaner there, but as she always refused to go into the building alone at night, he often had to accompany her. He agreed with Margaret, "This building is haunted".

THE GHOST BROUGHT HIS BRIEFCASE

Office cleaners are not usually given to flights of fancy or wild imaginings, so when Mrs Georgina Viney saw a gentleman in a suit and waistcoat, carrying a briefcase, wandering down a corridor in County Hall, Newport, she never dreamed he could be a ghost.

Georgina is now a cleaner at the County Press offices in Pyle Street, but for 14 years she worked the 5pm to 8pm shift at County Hall, cleaning offices on the fifth floor. It was there one evening, when most of the staff had gone home, that she and fellow cleaner Pearl, were working in a corridor.

Georgina could see Pearl cleaning the other side of a glass door, and noticed a man wearing a dark three-piece suit standing next to her."He seemed to be looking through the door at me and he was carrying a briefcase. Then he turned and walked away. I went over to Pearl and asked her whom she had been talking to. She just looked at me blankly and said she didn't know what I was on about."

Pearl had not seen the figure at all, although he had apparently been standing beside her, but over the years other people have seen the ghost with his briefcase roaming the corridors on the top floor. Georgina's successor there, Ann, saw him clearly, although the other cleaners had been careful not to speak of the ghost in case she was too frightened to take the job.

Hall-keeper at County Hall, Mr John Short, confirmed that the ghost had been reported on several occasions, although no-one knew why he should be there or indeed who he could be..... A very dedicated public servant perhaps who enjoyed his work so much that he came back from the grave!

The "new" five-storey extension to County Hall was built in the late 1960s on the site of Hazards House, a fine old 17th century building which had its own ghost; that of maidservant who killed herself in a "nasty dark cupboard" long ago.

She was seen - and felt - by Newport businesswoman Miss Audrey Spanner while on A.R.P duty during the war. Audrey actually stepped aside and apologised to the apparition which wore a long skirt, when she bumped into her on the stairs. Since the old house was demolished, the maid has not been encountered among desks and filing cabinets. She has been replaced by a ghost who appears much more at home in his surroundings.

THE HAUNTING OF HAZARDS TERRACE

Hazards Terrace in Newport's ancient Sea Street was aptly named because when the River Medina rose, the little brick cottages there would flood. But for the Bloomfield family, who lived in number sixty-two, the name held a far more sinister significance.

From the time they moved there in 1947 until they left almost thirty years later, strange things would happen. Locked and fastened doors opened by themselves, footsteps were heard crossing empty rooms, lamps were moved, and loud knocking and banging noises kept the children awake.

Brian Bloomfield, now a housing warden for Medina Borough Council, living at St John's Hill, Ryde, was a youngster of eight when he and his seven brothers and sisters moved into that house.

"Our mum just wouldn't believe there was anything going on there and refused to listen to us. But Dad knew differently and he would be the one who came in with the torch in the middle of the night when we had heard or felt something." In those days just after the war, there was no electricity upstairs and the family relied on oil lamps and candles for light, and coal fires for warmth. Brian recalls that the four-bedroom house always felt cold."However close you sat to the fire you never really got warm."

His most disturbing experience happened as he lay in bed one night and an icy cold hand touched his forehead. "I have never felt anything that cold before or since. As I lay there trembling with fright, something shuffled out of the room. I heard it move slowly down the stairs and leave by the back door."

Brian's elder sister, Mrs Betty Beeney, of Harding Road, Ryde, also has unpleasant memories of that old house. She recalls that for years, at 2.45am precisely each morning, there would be a creaking on the stairs, as if someone....or something.... was climbing up towards the sleeping family.

Then one day it happened. Her bedroom door opened and she saw the outline of a man standing there. "I screamed for my dad, but by the time he came running with his torch, it was gone," she said.

Whatever was haunting the old house also showed itself to young Brian one morning just as dawn was breaking. The grey-white shape which took on a man's figure was standing just by the door. As the boy watched, it vanished into thin air. Betty, too, experienced a touch from those freezing cold hands, and from then on she always insisted on sleeping in the middle of the double bed with her two sisters on the outside.

One night when a few of the children were alone in the house, they rushed in terror to their next door neighbour, Mrs Olive Hobbs, because something had been banging so violently on an old tin bath hanging on a wall that it shook the whole house.

Mrs Hobbs must have felt something was not quite right in the adjoining house because although she would drop in for a cuppa and a chat during the day, she would never set foot there after dark, recalled Betty.

An Unseen Presence

The old terrace was finally pulled down in 1988 to provide more parking space for County Hall. During the last years of its life, Hazards Terrace which had become increasingly dilapidated was used as temporary accommodation for the homeless.

At one time the cottages were owned by Miss Gubbins. She lived at nearby Hazards House, which was itself demolished to make way for the County Hall extension in the late 1960s. This too was haunted, and housekeeper Mrs Downer who lived on the premises, would often feel an unseen being pass her on the staircase in the 300-year-old house.

During the 1930s, number sixty-two was occupied by the Knight family, who left in 1938. However, Mr Len Knight of Highfield Road, Newport, recalled nothing more alarming than a succession of cockroaches migrating from the long-vanished Perkins bakery at the bottom of High Street. The family noticed no ghost during their time there, he said.

However, before the Bloomfields moved in, at least five people passed away in number sixty-two. Mrs Doris Hollowell, Len's older sister, said that their grandparents, a young brother and sister, and a subsequent tenant had all died in that house.

Whose was the restless spirit responsible for haunting the Bloomfields? With the house now reduced to rubble, it seems we shall never know.

With Hazards Terrace reduced to rubble, Len Knight stands in what was once his old home.
(Photograph courtesy of the IW County Press).

15

CHAPTER TWO

ISLAND ROADS <u>ARE</u> DIFFERENT!

THE GHOST WITH NO FACE

Janet Eldridge made it a rule never to pick up hitch-hikers. But one dark September night she foolishly broke that rule, with strange and terrifying consequences. As she drove across Staplers Heath towards Wootton, Janet was at peace with the world. The road ahead was empty. Then her headlights picked out the figure of a woman trudging along the grass verge a hundred yards ahead.

Thinking the stranger's car must have broken down, she slowed down to offer her a lift as it was dark and they were in the middle of nowhere.

Janet stopped her van and waited. The woman who was wearing a long skirt and had a shawl tightly wrapped around her head and shoulders, leaned across the bonnet and peered inside. "I pushed my window back thinking she was coming round to the door to ask for a lift. But she just walked off across the road and straight through the hedge. She was a ghost and I had been about to offer her a lift," gasped Janet.

More horrifying still, as she sat there trying to make sense of what she had seen, Janet realised the woman did not have a face. There was just a grey blankness where the features should have been. She started the van and took off for home, breaking all the speed limits on the way.

Still in a state of shock, she told her husband Des what had happened, and as she re-lived her ordeal, found herself growing hotter and hotter. "I felt as if I was on fire. I was burning all over. I could almost feel the flames licking up over my arms. I could hear them crackle. The intense heat was agonising. I cried out to Des, 'I am burning. Please do something'. I was terrified. I thought I was going to burst into flames and become one of those cases of spontaneous combustion."

Janet's ordeal lasted several minutes and neither the cool night air nor cold wet flannels lessened the burning sensation. When it was finally over, Janet slept, mercifully without dreams.

It was more than two years before she could bring herself to drive along that stretch of road again on her own, and she still cannot pass the spot where the ghost disappeared without a shudder.

"Who or what she was, I have no idea. She was obviously searching for something but she did not find it in my van. I sometimes wonder if perhaps she perished in a fire long ago and I caught an echo of this, somehow experiencing her last agonising moments as she burned."

COLLISION WITH A CAVALIER

One dark night as she was driving towards Godshill, Mrs Pat Pledge of Newport, saw a figure moving towards her car. She braked sharply but not in time to avoid a collision. The friend who was with her screamed and Pat braced herself for the impact. None came.

As she drove straight through the man, he simply vanished leaving both women in a state of shock. Pat can still recall every detail of that odd encounter because, as she soon realised, she had hit a ghost.

"All I could see was the top of his tunic which was dark with two rows of brass buttons down the front. He was wearing a black hat with a feather, and looked like a Civil War cavalier or Royalist. I just stopped the car and sat there, trembling," Pat recalled.

Stranger still, it was on this very same stretch of road, just past Bohemia Corner, that she had seen a phantom horse floating just above the highway, some months earlier. She had slowed right down so as not to frighten the animal, before noticing that its hooves were not touching the ground, and as Pat watched in astonishment, the grey horse drifted through a hedge and vanished.

"I am convinced there was some connection between the two and that they were probably horse and rider, but why I saw them several months apart, I will never know."

WRAITHS OF THE ROADS

Miles away in the village of Nettlestone, a woman in white is a well-known traffic hazard. Many motorists have rounded that corner by the village church only to find this ghost standing in the road.

Ted Jones was on his way home with lads from his local darts team one night when they literally ran into her. "We were in an old Buick and as we rounded the bend by the old church, there she was. We all saw her but Ken Scriven who was at the wheel couldn't stop in time, and we went right through her."

They searched the road but could find no body, so they drove into Ryde to report the accident to the police.

As the shaken young men stammered out their story, PC Harry Coffin just laughed. "We get quite a few reports of people knocking her down. Run along home, lads, you've just run over the White Lady of Nettlestone," he told them.

Another apparition has been seen at Vittlefields crossroads along the Forest Road, where motorists, including some police patrol riders, have swerved to avoid a young motor cyclist who has appeared suddenly in their path.

The shocked drivers were convinced the young man had been thrown from his machine and was lying badly injured, or dead, at the side of the road. They were right. He HAD been killed - many years earlier - during the last war, when, as a young dispatch rider, he collided with an army tank at that very spot.

....AND A BLACK DOG

As an experienced pilot with Trinity House, Edwin Bennett, had excellent night vision. Driving back from the West Wight late one evening, he struck a large black dog which came bounding across the road at his little sports car.

Certain he had badly injured if not killed the unfortunate beast, Edwin got out of the car and went to look for its body. He found nothing. A little further up the road he stopped at the local pub to ask if the landlord knew the owners of such a dog, so that he could contact them.

As he recounted his story, the regulars started to wink and nudge one another. They told Edwin he would never find the dog's body...for he had just hit a ghost-dog. Long, long ago the animal used to patrol the lonely cliffs with its master, a Preventive Officer, in search of smugglers, they said.

One dark night the pair came upon a band of smugglers and in the struggle that followed both man and dog were killed and their bodies thrown over the cliff. To this day the dog's ghost is still seen, but whether it is searching for its master or its murderers, who can say?

GHOST TRAIN

No train has run from Newport for well over 30 years, so when Mrs Kay Liggens of Freshwater, caught a glimpse of an old locomotive with three carriages steaming towards Cowes, it was a ghost-train she was seeing.

"It was only there for a few seconds. It seemed to be crossing an old brick viaduct near where the Newport to Cowes road is now. I heard nothing. The train was completely silent. It was as if it was in mid-air. I saw the steam train and two or three carriages but it was all so quick I could hardly believe it."

Kay and her husband had been walking down Holyrood Street one lunch-time and were standing by the brewery depot when she saw the apparition. "I just stood there, open-mouthed. I asked Roger when the last steam trains ran in Newport." "Not since the 1960's," he replied.

It was then Kay knew for certain, she had just glimpsed a ghost-train.

THE MILLER'S GHOST

The ghostly hunched figure of an old miller at Yafford still trudges across the road carrying a heavy sack on his back, at the dead of night.

Now a tourist attraction with a farm park, museum, waterfowl and rare breeds collection, Yafford Watermill, near Shorwell, offers a fascinating glimpse into the past. Some visitors may see much more than they ever expected - if the ghostly miller is there, grinding the corn.

A mill has probably stood on the site since the Middle Ages. The present building dates back to around 1740 and for over two centuries, its stones ground corn, barley and oats for local farmers. Until the mid 1960's the mill was still paying its way, but when the last miller, 'Stocky' Salter, finally retired in 1970, the business closed for good.

John Attrill has worked at Yafford Mill and lived in the old cottage next to the huge water-wheel, where he says he often felt a strong, but friendly presence, around the house. The ghost is sometimes fleetingly seen near the old mill pond and visitors occasionally remark that they have sensed or seen him about the place.

Two sightings happened several months apart, both at around 2am on clear moonlit nights. A local taxi driver from Brighstone taking visitors back to Brighstone Holiday Centre, saw a man's figure crossing the lane outside the mill, in front of the car. The ghost which was carrying a heavy sack, simply vanished as it reached the mill.

The same apparition, still with its burden, was also seen by John's grown-up son Roger, as he came home late one night. The description tallies in both cases, for Roger clearly saw a stooped figure with a weighty load on its shoulders traipsing across the lane to the mill .... the ghostly miller on his way to grind a sack of corn perhaps?

THEY CARRIED SKULLS

It was a blustery, wet September night when Joan and Peter Gunston left the Ponda-Rosa at Ashey (now the Tirol) to drive back to Bembridge. Regular visitors to the Island, they had enjoyed the dinner-dance, and it was approaching midnight as they made their way home along back lanes, past Hardingshute and Nunwell.

Joan and Peter of Corey's Mill, Stevenage, who are both retired, saw no other traffic, but as they rounded a left-hand bend, there, in the headlights, was a crowd of people dressed all in black. "There must have been fifty of them standing in the lane. They wore long hooded robes and several were brandishing poles adorned with rams' skulls," said Joan.

Peter brought the car to a halt, telling his wife to lock her door and window. The figures started milling around the car, peering in at the frightened pair.

"They made no sound at all. Their faces were completely hidden by the hoods. Several of them raised their hands and one passed a finger across its throat in a threatening gesture. We were extremely scared by this time and Peter decided to drive on," Joan said.

"We thought they would get out of the way when the car started to move but they continued to encircle us. Peter put his foot down and I thought we would hit them. Instead the car passed right through the figures.....they weren't solid at all. As we made contact with them they started to dissolve. After we had driven through the throng I looked back. The lane was completely empty."

Totally unnerved by their experience, Joan and Peter didn't stop to investigate further, but drove to Bembridge in a state of shock. They have never been down that lane since. "Who or what did we see that night? Could they have been the spirits of Devil worshippers or witches from long ago?" speculated Joan.

The Gunstons' experience may indeed be associated with the occult, for almost 400 years ago, in the reign of Queen Elizabeth 1, witchcraft was practised in Ashey. It is recorded in the Ryde Court Rules, known as the Ashey Papers, that Agnes Porter, a widow residing within the jurisdiction of the Lord of the Manor of Ashey was accused of being a witch and convicted. All her goods and chattels were forfeited to the Lord.

What did Joan and Peter witness that night in 1982? A dark and sinister echo from the Island's pagan past? .... They believe it was.

CHAPTER THREE

SOME HAUNTED FORTS

For centuries the Island has been a strategic point for invading forces looking for a bridgehead into mainland Britain. A defence network still stands - from the Spithead forts in the eastern Solent to the Needles Battery, Golden Hill Fort and Fort Redoubt which guard the western approaches.

GHOSTS OF GOLDEN HILL

Ivor Allison and his wife, Jill, have lived at Golden Hill Fort, Freshwater, since it was bought by Hayling Island businessman Mr Wilfred Perkins in 1984. The fort was almost derelict when they arrived and the couple have worked to build it into one of the Island's most unusual tourist attractions. They have become familiar with its maze of winding corridors and arched rooms, often welcoming back ex-servicemen who were once stationed there. Ivor and Jill have also come to know the fort ghosts. "One of them smokes a very sweet aromatic pipe and the aroma lingers in the corridor near our office in the early mornings or late at night when no visitors are around," Jill said.

"We often get people asking why there are servicemen in old-fashioned uniforms about. Last year, one lad saw a sailor leaning against a door in the room above the Colonnade tea room, and the same figure has also been seen lounging in the doorway with his pipe."

Built between 1863 and 1872 at a cost of £38,000, the six-sided brick barracks once housed 128 men and eight officers. Its guns were intended to cover the rear of the more vunerable coastal batteries from attack by the French. Regiments whose men have been stationed at Golden Hill include the Royal Artillery, Duke of Cornwall's Light Infantry, the IW Rifles, the Royal Hampshires and the Royal Militia of Jersey.

It is thought to be a sergeant-major from one of these regiments who fell, or was pushed to his death, during the First World War. Hated by his men, he plunged down one of the fort's two stone spiral staircases, breaking his neck. The "accident" was hushed up; with official reports stating he was 'killed in action'. His uniformed ghost has been seen on the roof and in the old officers' mess.

His fellow-phantom is an 19th century sailor, one of a small number of naval ratings stationed at Golden Hill. He, it is whispered, attempted to sell plans of the fort's defences to the French enemy. For his treason he was condemned to death and spent his last lonely hours before execution in one of the fort's prison cells.

An old iron hook to which the hangman's noose was fixed can still be seen. And the wooden trap through which the sailor dropped is still in place - now discreetly covered by a piece of carpet.

Ghost in the Tunnel

Brian Perkins had quite a fright at the fort one night in 1984, when he was clearing rubbish from one of the underground tunnels. Brian was helping with the renovations for his grandfather, Wilfred Perkins, the fort's new owner. He was still working at 11pm when he felt a hand on his shoulder.

"I spun round. There was no-one there. The tunnel was absolutely deserted but something had touched me. I ran back through the courtyard and locked myself in the office," he said. "I would not go there again after dark. It was a horrible place to walk round. There was a strange feel to it."

Ivor Allison remembers the incident well, because in his panic, Brian kicked the office door in, breaking the frame - although he had the key in his pocket. He managed to lock himself in, and was still there when Ivor found him.

The Old Prison Cell

A businesswoman who never believed in ghosts soon changed her mind when she moved to Golden Hill Fort to run the Colonnade Tea Rooms. Mrs Sheila Hughes of Norton Green would scoff at visitors who spoke of seeing the fort ghosts. To her it was all in the mind, or tales dreamed up to titillate the tourists - until one midsummer day in 1988, when she too saw a ghost and became an instant, if reluctant, believer.

Sheila, who has now given up the business, was in the back kitchen, once the fort's prison cells, where the double-barred windows and metal lined doors can still be seen. "Everything was quiet and the first visitors had yet to arrive," she said. "Suddenly I had a peculiar feeling that someone was

Did he fall or was he pushed down this twisting spiral staircase at Golden Hill Fort, Freshwater? Only his ghost knows and he isn't saying.

21

standing in the kitchen with me. I went very cold, and as I turned I glimpsed the figure of a man standing beside me. I couldn't make out his features or what he was wearing. He disappeared as suddenly as he had come, leaving behind a feeling of chill and foreboding.

"I was icy cold, yet outside the sun was shining and it was a warm morning. I firmly believe there is a presence in that building and it is a very disturbed one. He transmitted a very strong feeling of despair and fear."

Sheila is convinced Golden Hill Fort is not a lucky place. "Things go wrong there for no reason. It was folly to build it."

The Pub Ghost

With almost 25 years in the Royal Navy behind him, Alan Burgess is not a credulous man. But the landlord of the fort's pub, the Lord Palmerston, has both seen and spoken to a ghost.

"One night I was cashing up, when a man walked past the bar and down the stone passageway towards the toilets. Thinking it was the fort manager, I called out, but he ignored me. Then I noticed the air had become incredibly cold and the temperature had dropped dramatically. I searched the place, but found no-one there. I remember the figure had on a white shirt or tunic. I only saw its reflection in the mirror."

The pub has a cold spot just inside the stone passageway, and behind the wooden panelling is a dumb waiter lift at which visitors' dogs bark and howl. Before taking on the pub in 1988, Alan ran an exhibition in one of the first floor rooms. Here the temperature would often drop very suddenly and the room would grow icy cold. Alan never saw the ghost although he felt its presence; it was in this part of the fort that the treacherous sailor was hanged.

The Door Swung Open

More than 20 years ago Maureen Sutton of Freshwater, worked at Golden Hill Fort for local lampshade makers Readers Fancicraft. One night when she was there alone, finishing an order, she heard footsteps in the room with her. The unseen visitor came closer and closer.

"My nerve broke and I ran. I was in such a panic that I fell over and cut my head. With blood trickling down my face, I got out into the courtyard - and then I smelled pipe smoke in the cold evening air."

On another occasion, Maureen and several other girls took their coffee break out on the verandah. As they sat chatting over steaming mugs, heavy steel bolts on the stairway door slid back by themselves and the door swung open. "The five of us jumped up, spilling hot coffee down our legs. Then we realised that whatever had opened the door, had been on the verandah with us."

"Strange things would happen at the fort, but we grew used to the ghosts. Articles in the workshop would disappear; whatever was haunting the fort had a streak of naughtiness. We would lift bags of fabric and find the bottoms ripped open. One day, an old alarm clock which had no works inside, started to tick loudly," said Maureen.

In an engineering workshop below, now the Lord Palmerston pub, one of the workers often saw the ghost of the unfortunate sergeant-major, who would march in whenever he was working late. The man recognised the spectral soldier and would pass the time of day with him, but refused to tell Maureen the phantom's name, because he said the dead officer's family still lived in the West Wight.

CONCERT FROM BEYOND THE GRAVE

A dozen regimental police are not easily frightened. But one night spent in the empty officers' quarters near Golden Hill Fort was more than they could stand. By 2am they were so unnerved by their experiences in the old building that they took to their heels and ran.

Gerald Wildish, of Tennyson Road, Cowes, remembers it well. He was stationed at the fort for his National Service from 1959 to 1962 with the R.A.S.C., learning about seamanship, handling boats and landing craft.

By then the fort's days were numbered, and Gerald's regiment, the last troops to be stationed on the Island, were preparing to move out. "It was a bleak, grim place," he recalled. "There were so few men left that twelve regimental police were brought in to do guard duties."

That cold, clear night in early spring, Gerald was standing his last night's guard duty. The reinforcements had arrived that afternoon, drawn their bedding, and were camping out in the empty officers' quarters across the road. At 11pm the huge fort gates were closed; Gerald and five other men settled down for their watch. At just after 2am came a tremendous disturbance. There was shouting, running footsteps and a hammering at the fort gates.

All twelve regimental police, including a sergeant and four corporals, were outside the main gates in a state of undress, shouting to be let in. Gerald woke the duty cook, who brewed strong tea for the shaken men.

"They refused to go back to the officers' quarters that night and slept in the fort cells instead. They told us they had all heard classical piano music being played in the empty building. At first they thought it was someone fooling around, but the music continued. They searched the place - but there wasn't a stick of furniture there, let alone a grand piano.

"Finally their nerve broke and they ran, wearing whatever uniform came to hand. We discovered later that the building may have been used in 1957 as a temporary mortuary for some of the dead from the Island's worst-ever air disaster," said Gerald.

This involved a Short Solent flying boat owned by Aquila Airways, which crashed shortly after take-off from Southampton, killing 45 people. It came down in a chalk pit at Shalcombe Farm and burst into flames. Two officers from Golden Hill Fort and a senior NCO were just yards away when the plane crashed; they led the rescue party dragging out dead and injured, until, with their own clothing alight, they were driven back.

"The passengers had been flying to Madeira via Lisbon, and among the dead was a concert pianist on his way to an engagement," said Gerald. Did his spirit linger in the old deserted building until he could find an audience for his final concert from beyond the grave? Those twelve men certainly believed it did.

The old officers' quarters have since been converted into flats, but the ghostly pianist has given no encore. Occasionally, the sound of footsteps can heard in an empty apartment, but they bother nobody. One resident wistfully wished the pianist would make a comeback. "Imagine having your very own concerts given by a ghost. I would love it," she sighed.

THE HUNGRY GHOST

Over 90 years ago, four soldiers died in an horrific explosion at Fort Redoubt, Freshwater Bay, and at least one of them does not lie easy in his grave at a nearby churchyard. His ghost has been seen walking the casemates of the old garrison, searching it is said, for his dead comrades.

Perched on the cliff edge overlooking the bay, Fort Redoubt is now privately owned by Margit and Paddy Longmore, who run a thriving tea room built on the site of the old gun emplacements. The Redoubt was constructed in 1856 to protect against attack by the French, but its 12-pounder guns, which had a range of two miles, never fired a shot in anger.

The garrison could accommodate more than 30 men and officers and, in 1860, Queen Victoria and the young Princess Beatrice were entertained to tea there by the colonel's wife. More than 40 years later, during artillery practice in front of senior officers on June 25 1901, the breech block of the fort's right hand gun blew out, killing Captain Arthur LeMesurier Bray, Gunner Charles Dorman, Gunner Rickets, and Bombardier Macdonald, also injuring several other men.

By 1918 the fort was totally disarmed and sold by the War Office ten years later for £600. In 1970 it was bought by an American millionaire, Byron DeWitt Daugherty. The present owners purchased it in 1977 and opened the tea room seven years later. Margit and Paddy love their unusual home with its a peaceful and relaxing atmosphere but they are certain that ghosts still walk in the old fort.

Two phantom soldiers have been seen standing on the bridge over the deep ditch which surrounds the redoubt. One of them is smoking a cigarette. Whilst in the entrance tunnel, there lurks the dark shadow of another soldier said to have been crushed to death against the wall by a horse and cart.

An eerie green light can sometimes be glimpsed as it flickers around the courtyard before disappearing into the former guard room, while some old Freshwater fishermen will not go near the fort after dark. The Longmores are certain their ghosts have a sense of humour - and a fondness for things electrical - especially video recorders which go haywire.

Unable to sleep one night, Margit got up at 3am, made herself a coffee, and went back to bed. As she drifted off to sleep, she glanced at her radio alarm. The digital display showed it was 7am, so she got up, washed and dressed, ready to start the day.

"A ghost was having a joke at my expense because when I started work I found it was still the middle of the night. That electric clock had been put forward four hours," Margit said.

Her cat and dog see something in the fort which is invisible to human eyes and often stare very intently at it. While in the tea-room itself, a greedy

Perched on the cliff edge overlooking Freshwater Bay, the ghosts of soldiers killed at Fort Redoubt still walk.

ghost has been heard smacking its lips over the choice of cakes. "My daughter and a waitress were trying to decide which of the gateaux looked the most delicious, before the customers arrived. My daughter thought she liked the lemon cake the best."

"Mmmmmm", someone sighed with longing. Both girls spun round but the room was empty.... Whatever was in there with them, had certainly sounded hungry.

TWO TRAGEDIES AT SANDOWN

Although no shot was ever fired in anger from its granite walls, a young soldier was cut in two in an horrific accident at the old Sandown Fort. His ghost has been seen in the years since his agonising death, and Jack Corney, owner of the IW Zoo which now occupies the former fort, does not disbelieve the sightings by some of his keepers and zoo staff.

The fort was built between 1861 and 1866 as part of the Island's defences against a possible French invasion, but the four officers and 67 men stationed there never saw action and it was later decommissioned. The present zoo, with its world-renowned snake and venom centre, opened in the 1978, with tigers and bears in place of soldiers.

After hearing tales of the soldier's ghost, Jack looked into the fort's history and discovered an inquest report into the tragedy dating back to 1888. The fort's guns were massive and when fired, the recoil was absorbed by the wheeled mounts they rested upon. A number of soldiers were carrying out maintenance when the rope holding a gun barrel slipped. As the 18-ton gun started to roll backwards, the sergeant in charge jumped clear.

He shouted a warning to the soldier working under the gun, but it came too late. The unfortunate man was caught half way out. Slowly the heavy gun slid backwards, cutting him in two.

In the century since then, his ghost has been seen in the fort and near the moat. Something tampers with the electric lights in the old fort tunnels, and Jack, a man who breeds tigers and handles some of the world's most deadly snakes, has to agree - there is sometimes a very spooky feeling in the fort, especially near that old gun emplacement.

An earlier quadrangular barracks at Sandown, built near Sandham Gardens in 1632, was also the scene of a tragedy when a master gunner went insane. He shot his wife and child, and after threatening to blow up the fort, cut his own throat.

The self-inflicted injury was not fatal, and he was still able to put himself under arrest. It would be interesting to know if any ghostly echoes of this tragedy are still felt there today.

Remains of the original fort buildings can still be seen at the IW Zoo, Sandown, where a young gunner was cut in half.

CHAPTER FOUR

ADVENTURES IN TIME

THE PUB THAT VANISHED

One dark November night, Laurie West set out from Newtown with a friend for what turned out to be the strangest night of their lives. On that cold wet evening ten years ago, they came upon a pub that doesn't exist and shared a drink with some very unsociable spirits.

Laurie lives and works at Ryde. A rational Islander in his forties, he is still puzzled by his experiences that night which, years later, remain etched in his memory. He has made every effort to find that old pub again and has spent many hours driving the lanes around Calbourne trying to locate it. He has undertaken historical research in the county archives in an effort to trace it, to no avail, and has questioned local people as to its whereabouts. But Laurie has reached the inescapable conclusion that he had been drinking in a ghost-pub.

The pub was called The Vulcan or The Falcon. "I don't remember which, because it did not seem significant at the time," said Laurie. "I picked up my friend at Newtown and we set out to have a drink. As we were driving towards Shalfleet, I noticed a lane on our left and asked my companion if he had ever been down it.

"I thought later it was odd that my friend did not recognise the turning, because he had lived in the area for many years. Some way down the lane we saw a pub on the right and pulled onto the gravelled area at the front. The pub signboard was swinging and creaking in the wind, way up high over the door.

"We went in through a small porch and tried the lounge bar first. This was full of heavy, brown leather furniture, and was deserted. There was an unpleasant chilly feeling, so we made for the public bar instead."

Laurie recalls that this bar had a flagstone floor, a large, empty and cold fireplace, wooden tables and chairs. The whole atmosphere was cheerless and unfriendly. A drably-dressed woman was serving behind the bar, and there were about fifteen other people in the room, all middle-aged or older and wearing rather shabby, old-fashioned clothes.

Everybody Stopped Talking.....

"Everybody stopped talking and stared as we came in. It was rather unnerving. They continued to watch as we got our drinks. I asked for a gin and ginger beer - somebody had suggested I should try it. The barmaid said, 'We don't have that.' So I said I would have gin and ginger ale instead. It was actually quite horrible. We sat down at one of the tables. The people around us had resumed their conversations, but they kept glancing at us. We felt like intruders. We were not at all welcome."

He recalls paying for the drinks with a pound note and being given change in florin and shilling coins, which did not strike him as unusual, since they doubled as 10p and 5p pieces in decimal coinage.

With no fire in the large fireplace, the bar felt cold. Laurie and his friend sipped their drinks, feeling more and more uncomfortable. "We certainly didn't want another so we left. I could hardly wait to get out of the place and I was aware that every pair of eyes in the room followed our departure."

They hurried out into the night with a feeling of relief, and driving out of the deserted car park Laurie could see the pub sign still swinging and creaking in the wind.

"We drove a short way down the road and were amazed to find ourselves at the Sun Inn, Calbourne. It just wasn't possible. We had not crossed the main Newport-Yarmouth road at any point. I thought at the time it was strange that the two pubs should have been so close together."

The two men had one drink there and then Laurie dropped his friend back at Newtown and drove home to Ryde, still puzzling about that unfriendly pub. The whole episode had so disturbed him that a few days later he decided to go back in daylight and try to discover why it felt so unwelcoming.

"I never found the pub again. I drove all over the place trying to retrace our steps. That lane just did not exist. Eventually I went to the little village shop in Calbourne and asked if there was another pub nearby. The answer was, 'No'."

Next, Laurie inquired at the County Records Office about old pubs in the area but drew yet another blank. After hearing his story, the archivist told Laurie he must have had a few too many that night, because there was no such place. So the mystery remains. Both Laurie and his friend were at the pub that night. They felt at the time that something was very wrong. Now they know why. The Vulcan or Falcon just doesn't exist. Not in this world or dimension, anyway......

TRAVELLER IN TIME

An old Victorian house in Wootton still haunts the dreams of electrical engineer Mr Dan Cox of Clarence Road, East Cowes, for it was there some 20 years ago that he travelled back in time and glimpsed his home as it was in the 1920s.

It was an incredible and terrifying experience for Dan, who, even now, is unable to understand or explain it, but can recall details of that winter's night with startling clarity. "It was no dream, that I do know, but whether I actually slipped back in time or saw some kind of ghost house, I will never be sure."

Dan, then twenty, moved to the Island with his parents and younger brother George in 1968, to an unfurnished flat in The Brannons, a large Victorian house in Station Road near the Woodman's Arms pub. The family had a spacious apartment on the ground floor. The rooms were grand, with high ceilings, and what had once been the lounge or withdrawing room had been divided into two bedrooms. Dan and George shared one, and their parents had the adjoining room.

It was one bright moonlight night when Dan awoke at 2am with a feeling that something was dreadfully wrong. Glancing over to where George should have been, he saw a large, grey upholstered sofa instead.

Thinking he must still be dreaming, he turned over in bed only to find the partition wall had gone, and in place of his parents' bed, he saw the glowing embers of a dying fire in an old-fashioned cast-iron grate.

"I was wide awake by this time," said Dan. "At first I was puzzled, but as the seconds ticked by, I began to panic. This was the room as it would have been 50 years ago. My parents and brother had disappeared. Where was I ?"

Dan was no longer conscious of his own body and could not see his bed."I felt no sensation. There was no sound, and the room felt neither cold nor warm. There was a clock on the mantlepiece, but it made no sound, and the fire emitted no heat, no crackle of burning coals."

Looking desperately around the strange room, Dan noticed that the walls were now covered with leafy patterned wallpaper, and it looked as if electricity had been newly installed in the house as there was a hanging glass lampshade in the centre of the room in place of the partition, and cable had been fixed on top of the wallpaper. "Working with electrics, I notice these things," Dan explained. He also remembers a large piano or bureau against one wall. As the seconds passed and the room did not waver or change, Dan wondered if he should get up and explore the rest of the house. But......

"I could not bring myself to get out of bed. I froze at the thought I might never find the bed again and be somehow trapped in a time before I was born."

He closed his eyes tight and concentrated on feeling his body return again, then turned back into his original position. When he opened his eyes, George was there once more in place of the sofa and the room had returned to normal.

Dan still believes that he drifted back in time for those few minutes. It has never happened to him again. But even now, if he wakes in the middle of the night, he opens his eyes very, very carefully......

THE BLOODSTAINED FOOTPRINTS

The Mystery of the Bloodstained Footprints and The Shadow at the Window sound like a couple of thrillers. Great titles for plays perhaps, at the Trinity Theatre, Cowes. But if the actors are not careful they sometimes find the theatre ghost literally getting in on the act and trying to steal the show.

The 249-seat theatre, set back from Bath Road, is the permanent home of the Cowes Amateur Operatic and Dramatic Society otherwise known as CAODS, who are quite used to the pranks of their ghost. It is company policy that all the props must be checked before every performance, as they have a nasty habit of disappearing or being moved around the stage.

The ghost is such an accepted part of the company that it even stars regularly in Stage Whisper, the CAODS monthly magazine. Tony and Rosie Collard produce the cartoons which are always about the current production, and each one starts: "Trinity Spook Says....."

Chris Buckett is the Theatre Club manager who also doubles as theatre technician and a stage manager. A member of the company since 1975, he is a firm believer in the ghost, having heard and seen it on several occasions.

Supernatural activity in the theatre seems to be centred around a storage room in the north west corner of the building, and in the lighting box above. When Chris first saw the ghost, it was standing in the doorway to that room one summer evening, dressed all in black. He shouted, "Can I help you?" The figure vanished. Since then it has been seen by other members of the company, always in the same doorway.

Trinity Theatre's bloodstained footprints which sometimes disappear.

Trinity Theatre's stage.

An Unnatural Cold

That room is always cold, an unnatural cold some say, even in midsummer when the rest of the theatre is hot and airless. Leading up to the lighting box is a wooden ladder which Chris will never go up if he is alone in the theatre. He admits he feels afraid there.

Even when that tiny room is locked and empty, figures have been seen moving between windows which resemble eyes high up in the wall. People in the audience often find their gaze being drawn there. Whenever Chris climbs into the lighting box, he has a strong presentiment that he is going to find a man hanging from the roof rafter, but so far the room has been empty......

Several years ago a cast iron fireplace was needed as a prop in a forthcoming production. Chris's brother, Michael, and three friends volunteered to collect it. All four men struggled to lift the heavy fireplace onto the stage, but when they turned away to build the rest of the set, that fireplace jumped off the stage, landed several yards away in the auditorium, and shattered.

Then there is the mystery of the footprints which come and go for no apparent reason. They were first noticed when the wooden floor was scrubbed clean after the theatre had been used by London-based Juliana's nightclub as part of the Cowes Week festivities in 1979. Before the seats were replaced, the huge dark footprints faded away then reappeared, weaving their way across the wooden boards. Some days they are visible, at other times there is nothing to be seen.

A psychic friend who investigated the old theatre, declared that the footprints which lead from the back store room were made by blood which had soaked into the floor. When he attempted to stand on a pair of the prints he was knocked to the ground by some unseen, but very powerful, force.

He told Chris they had been made by a man who died in the building, possibly when it was used as a Red Cross and WRVS station for those injured in the blitz during the last war.

....And Impossible Footsteps

Chris has attempted to research the history of the old theatre but has met with little success. Records and deeds prior to 1958 were apparently destroyed in a fire, and church officials have politely, but firmly, refused to discuss the hall's past with him.

All he knows is that it was put up in 1914 as a hall for Holy Trinity Church, on the site of The Grove, a large house built in 1833 for Mrs Sarah Goodwin, who financed the building of Holy Trinity Church as a place of worship for 'sailors and seafarers' - and as a living for her cleric son-in-law.

An old iron fire escape on the side of the building, since removed to make way for an extension, is said to have been the scene of a death many years before, but again Chris has been unable to discover the details.

Footsteps are often heard in the empty theatre. They move down the centre of the auditorium to and from the stage - which is impossible, because there is no central aisle. Chris and other members of CAODS hear them, but the sound is only apparent when few people are about. Curiously for a theatre ghost, this one seems shy of appearing before an audience.

The footsteps may belong to a ghostly guest artiste who treads the boards at Trinity because his own theatre has disappeared. Albert DuBois recited monologues at the old Shanklin Pier Theatre in the 1890s but passed away after only his second season there. In the century since, however, he has made several come-backs. Performers in the old theatre heard his footsteps, always seven of them, coming up onto the stage. There were even plans to issue the ghost with his own Equity card!

When the old pier theatre closed its fittings were sold, and in 1979 those plush red velvet seats went to.... the Trinity Theatre, where it would appear that Albert's ghost still treads the boards.

MESSY LITTLE POLTERGEIST

Next to the Trinity Theatre, in Beken's Photographic shop, George the poltergeist still makes mischief. Although the old shop in Bath Road was exorcised by a vicar from Holy Trinity Church more than twenty years ago, the service was clearly not a success.

Whether a link exists between the theatre ghosts and George, no-one knows. Ros Booker, who has run the shop for more than thirty years, is accustomed to George and his antics, becoming quite concerned if she has not heard from him for a time.

Handbags and camera bags are his speciality. He loves to throw them about the shop if they are left on a particular shelf. Many years ago when the premises were run by Miss Burland, who sold fashion goods and yachting accessories, she would often complain that the poltergeist, which she described as a "nasty, naughty little thing", had left dirt and mess there during the night.

Displays of handbags would be sent flying so often that eventually in 1960, the local minister was summoned to cleanse the shop of its unwanted spirit.

George, however, refused to budge and when Bekens took over the premises, filling them with film and camera equipment, he happily switched his attentions to the camera bags stacked on shelves overhead.

"I often came in to find bags on the floor, and even now, as I am serving, the odd bag will be thrown off the shelf right across the shop," said Ros.

The same psychic who investigated the nearby theatre was also interested in George's activities. Could he be the ghost of a mail-coach driver? He wondered, throwing bags out as he passed staging posts, such as the one at the gates to The Grove where the shop now stands.

Whoever George once was, Ros is sure he is perfectly harmless and enjoys having him around. "I sometimes have to tell him off if he starts to throw things, but otherwise he is a happy little soul."

CHAPTER FIVE

GHOSTS WITH REGULAR HABITS

Some ghosts are only seen on particular days or at certain times of the year....

ONLY ON A FRIDAY

The outline of a severed hand and the word Friday carved into an old oak beam at a cottage in Roud, near Godshill, were treated as curiosities by Peter and Ann Moreton when they moved there in 1976. They should have known better.....

Rose Cottage has a very tranquil and welcoming atmosphere. A delightful place, built from old grey stone in the early 1700s, it stands on the site of a much earlier dwelling once in tithe to nearby Great Appleford.

When the couple moved to Rose Cottage with daughters Charlotte and Elizabeth, they were all entranced, and delighted in showing visitors the carving on a beam above the open fireplace. A man's huge left hand with fingers splayed had been traced and carved there, together with the name William Fleming and a date, FRIDAY 22 March 1774. The words "He that hath given to the poor leadeth to the LORD" are also carved in old-fashioned script in the beam.

Shortly after moving in, Peter and Ann noticed that all was not as it should be at Rose Cottage. As they sat chatting with friends in front of the log fire, everyone suddenly stopped talking, and listened. There in the lounge with them was the sound of water being poured from a jug onto the floor, although there was nothing to see.

Strange things would always happen on Fridays. The whole cottage would be filled with a feeling of foreboding. Lights would flicker and go out. The power would fail. Bathroom taps would be turned full on. Things got so bad, that on Fridays, Ann would take the children to her in-laws until Peter came home from work.

The little girls spoke of bright lights and a figure in their bedrooms, and Charlotte claimed to have seen a girl aged about ten with long blonde hair, standing in her parents' room one day.

The family's dog would sit at the top of the staircase watching something invisible to a human eye as it passed by on the stairs, and Peter's brother-in-law Graham, also found his attention drawn there when he came to stay. He had often slept on the settee downstairs at Rose Cottage but never spoke of what he had seen, in case it worried the family. However one night he rang Peter to say he had just attended a seance. Never having been to one before he had been more than a little surprised when a voice claiming to be that of a Brother John had tried to contact him.

This, it appeared, was the ghostly monk who regularly walked up and down the staircase at Rose Cottage when Graham was staying there. Brother John told him the cottage had once been called Rose Hill and that he had worked there as a stonemason almost 600 years ago.

Fridays continued to be bad days and Ann dreaded them. An almost

Did this outline of a severed hand carved on an old oak beam belong to William Fleming?

Why did bad things always happen at Rose Cottage on Fridays?

tangible, unpleasant feeling pervaded the cottage but only on a Friday. Then she discovered why......

The Hand in the Mirror

"I was sitting at my mirror putting my make-up on before going to work when I saw a hand behind me. It was a large fleshy man's hand which had been severed at the wrist; the edges were jagged and bloody," she said.

"I froze. I was petrified. Then something in me said, 'enough is enough'. I lost control and swore at it, telling it in no uncertain terms to go away, then closed my eyes. When I opened them again the hand was still there, but suddenly it vanished with a sort of 'wooshing' noise and somehow I knew it would not be coming back."

From that day on, Fridays haven't been a problem. The cottage feels at peace and if Brother John still wanders up and down the stairs, he bothers no-one.

All Peter and Ann occasionally notice now is the smell of aromatic tobacco coming from a corner of the lounge by the settee. Perhaps it is old William Fleming enjoying a quiet pipe at the end of a hard day.

THE PHANTOM FARRIER

A phantom farrier still works at his anvil forging iron shoes for ghostly horses at a lonely Brighstone farm. Sounds of hammering and the ring of metal on metal can be heard, along with the snorting and stamping of the animals waiting to be shod.

Chilton Farm, which stands just off the Military Road, is recorded in the Domesday Book. The present farmhouse was built in the early 1600s after an earlier house burnt down. Since 1971, it has been the home of farmers Sue and Richard Fisk, and subsequently their children, Jeremy and Victoria.

The house itself is haunted by the sad little shade of a young girl who lived her short life there and died at the tender age of twelve, over 100 years ago. "We never knew her name, we would just hear her weeping. The sound always seemed to come from one of the bedrooms, but whenever we went upstairs to look, it would suddenly stop," said Sue.

There was often a strong feeling of sadness in the far sitting room from which the little girl's weeping originated. Cilla Worsfold, Sue's younger sister, also heard that crying - a sound she cannot forget. Perhaps the little ghost child cried because she was lonely, for nothing has been heard of her since Jeremy and Victoria were born.

Outside, in barns and stables now converted into compact little holiday cottages, things are not so peaceful. Guests staying in one particular cottage have complained of being woken by a loud banging and hammering which seems to come from one of the old stone walls.

Within two seasons of taking visitors, no fewer than three mainland couples had told Sue of the weird noises. "I asked my visitors as they were leaving whether they had enjoyed their stay. They said it had been very nice, apart from the noise - a tremendous banging which had kept them awake two nights running."

One woman told Sue she had actually seen the ghost of a farrier at work with hammer and anvil making the horseshoes in a corner of the bedroom. A couple of months later, two more guests mentioned they had been kept awake by similar loud noises coming from a corner of the bedroom two nights running, although strangely no-one in the adjoining cottages had heard a sound.

The following autumn, two girls holidaying in the same cottage checked out a day early. They had enjoyed their stay, they said - apart from the noises. The girls admitted that two nights in a row they had been woken by banging and hammering, and the sound of animals moving around. The noises seemed to be coming from the next door cottage which they knew was unoccupied and they had ventured outside with torches to look for burglars.

The ghostly farrier works only on Friday and Saturday nights. Sue has even considered sleeping in the cottage herself to see if she can hear him. "The only trouble is none of us has the nerve to stay there at night," she admitted.

"What we cannot fathom is why he is only heard on those nights, and why people sleeping in adjoining cottages are not disturbed. It really is most strange."

The phantom farrier was once a man of flesh and blood who made shoes for the farm's shire horses and hunters. While excavating the old stone stables and barns, Sue and Richard discovered a number of ancient and rusting horseshoes under the floor of what had once been a smithy.

Although the last of the farm's working horses has long since died, the ghostly farrier works on...... forging shoes for those spectral animals.

A CRY AT CHRISTMAS

Late on Christmas Eve when their own children are tucked up in bed dreaming of Santa Claus, Mark and Tracy Grabham hear the patter of tiny feet on the stairs and a little voice calling,"Mummy, Mummy".

They have learned to take no notice, for the young girl is a ghost. She calls out at intervals for about twenty minutes on December 24th every year, at around 10.30pm. "It is a sleepy, plaintive little cry and it comes from the empty staircase," said Mark.

The young couple moved into their council house at Winston Road, Newport, in 1987, and this strange occurrence has happened every year since. Only three days after settling in, Tracy saw the ghost of a woman holding a baby in one of the bedrooms and childrens' footsteps could be heard in empty rooms overhead.

One afternoon, Mark came home to an empty house to hear children laughing. But as he stepped inside, the sound stopped abruptly. A quick search showed the house really was deserted - Tracy and the girls had gone to Ryde.

Mark recently saw the face of one of the little-ghost children peering at him from the bottom of the stairs. A girl aged about two, she smiled sweetly, then vanished.

Now every Christmas Eve while the children excitedly await Father

Christmas and their presents, Mark and Tracy are listening out instead for the cry of their little Christmas spirit.

SPIRIT ON VACATION

For more than fifty years the ghost of an aviator dropped in at the Brading guest house where he had spent many happy holidays. Every September the long-dead pilot would appear in his old room, much to the surprise of the current guests, and there he would stay for exactly a month.

Morton Farm still takes visitors and Graham Redfern who runs the 17th century guest-house with his wife Pat, is the fifth generation of his family to live there. He can recall the annual arrival of the ghost-pilot, and also remembers how the phantom who had outstayed his welcome, was sent packing by the Bishop of Portsmouth in 1958.

The clergyman was called in by Graham's exasperated mother who was tired of the presence and of having her guests disturbed by the holidaying ghost. "Whenever he was here, you could smell his cigar smoke. Doors would open and shut in front of you. We would hear the sound of heavy boots walking across the landing overhead and there was a sensation of someone - or something - in the room. It could be quite awkward as he continued to use his old room, startling the guests when he opened and closed locked doors. He would stay just for the month. When September came he would arrive and at the end of the month he would disappear again for another year."

The pioneer aviator was an Australian who always flew his biplane from London to the Island, landing at Morton Common. But one September, he crashed-landed and was killed. It seems his ghost was still determined to enjoy its annual holiday and did so, regularly, for a number of years until the Bishop carried out his exorcism.

These rites were a partial success. The pilot has never flown back since. But they had no effect on young Andrew, the ghost child who still lingers in the oldest part of the house. He died of diptheria more than a century ago at the age of eight, but his shade is still seen by sensitive guests who stay at the old farm.

"He is a sweet little lad and he always pays us a visit when we are here," one woman who has been a regular visitor for almost 20 years told Graham. "He just stands there in the corner of the room in his nightshirt and smiles at us."

Pepper, a little Jack Russell terrier which once belonged to Graham's grandfather, is occasionally seen sitting at the top of the stairs near the front door. Killed in an accident with a threshing machine many years ago, Pepper has returned.

"I sometimes see him sitting there as I walk through the hall. He has a bent ear, a black patch on one eye and he appears rather like a two-dimensional reflection," said Graham with a smile.

"We don't tell all our guests that we have the occasional ghost here in case it alarms them. But most of our regulars know, and they all love the warm and friendly atmosphere here.... It certainly drew the pilot back year after year."

THE APRIL GHOST

It is always April when the ghost of Orme House walks. An elderly lady wearing a long skirt, bodice, shawl and little leather boots has been seen walking in mid-air several feet above the bedroom floor where young Jessica Rainey was sleeping.

Jessica was almost ten when she awoke in the early hours to see the little old woman's shade in Georgian costume standing by one of her bedroom windows. She did not appear solid but seemed composed of tiny dots of light. "At first the lady was facing the wall, but she turned and walked over the top of me across the room. I lay very still, pretending to be asleep, and when I plucked up the courage to turn over, she had vanished," Jessica said.

When she told her parents, Mike and Sheila Rainey, the following morning, they said she must have been dreaming. However, exactly seven years later, on April 9 1992, when Jessica's younger sister, Laura, was sleeping in that same bedroom, she too saw a ghost.

"We had never told her of Jessica's experience because we knew she would be frightened, so when Laura started screaming at three o'clock that morning, sobbing that there was a ghost in her room, we were taken aback," said Mike.

Laura, then aged eleven, saw the head and shoulders of a figure outlined in a bright white light standing by her bedroom door and dived under her duvet until it had gone.

Orme House, a charming period home in the heart of Newport, was once three tiny cottages. One was rebuilt in the late 1700s to give the property a finer facade. It is in this section that the ghost is seen, moving in mid-air where she appears to be standing at the level of the old attic floor.

After Laura's brief glimpse of the ghost, the family checked old diaries and calendars to pinpoint her sister's earlier sighting and were disconcerted to find this occurred at 3am on April 9, 1985.

What is the significance of this date? The Rainey family are now researching the house's history to see what they can discover. Meanwhile, they have already put a ring around April 9 on their new year's calendar and a note which reads 'Look Out For Ghost.'

CHAPTER SIX

HAUNTED CAFES AND SHOPS

THE FISH AND CHIP SHOP PHANTOM

For over half-a-century, Stevens fish restaurant in Carisbrooke High Street was one of the best known on the Island, until Mr Ray Stevens hung up his apron and retired at Christmas 1991. But how many customers realised that the restaurant was haunted and that they were eating their fish and chips under the envious eye of a hungry ghost? Some staff were too frightened to work there late at night, and Ray, who still lives in part of the premises, has heard and sensed a presence many times, both by day and by night.

The cottages which formed the shop and restaurant are at least 200 years old, and have in their time been an undertaker's and a bakery. When Ray moved there with his family in 1938, strange things started to happen. Door handles would turn, doors would open, and something unseen would walk across the room. "When I was a nipper, I would stand and wait for the door to open and try to catch whatever it was. I never managed it," said Ray ruefully.

He is certain the ghost is an old woman, but has seen her only once. Until he carried out some alterations, she would be heard coming down the attic stairs, across a room, and down the next staircase. Doors would open as the ghost moved through the house with a heavy, purposeful tread.

After living with her for so long, Ray was taken completely by surprise late one night in 1984 when she went absolutely wild. Luckily, all the customers had gone and the restaurant was closed for the night.

On display was a new range of toys which Ray was selling, including some mechanical singing birds in cages. "Suddenly, and for no reason, everything started up, jigging and spinning round. The toys were going crazy. It was absolute pandemonium and we were all very frightened. Then, as suddenly as it had begun, it stopped. The restaurant was silent; the toys just toys again."

Heather Trevett of Carisbrooke, who worked for Ray for eleven years, remembers that night clearly. "The restaurant was closed and I was cashing up. I heard glasses in the rack above the bar start to clink, moving together, faster and faster, then the toy parrots in their cages started spinning round and round; for a few seconds the whole place went crazy. Suddenly it ceased. It was really eerie. I couldn't get out fast enough," Heather said with a shudder.

"She was a mischievous old ghost. You could usually tell when she was around for she certainly liked to watch us work. Quite often she would knock books off shelves and set them falling like rows of dominoes. Shelf after shelf of books would tumble to the floor."

Occasionally customers would ask if the restaurant was haunted. Some sensed a presence - one which obviously liked to linger there amid the diners and savour the smell of their fish and chips.

WATCHER ON THE STAIR

For 40 years or more, most of the customers at the Paramount Cafe in Shanklin Old Village have enjoyed meals, snacks or a cup of tea, quite unaware they may have been sharing a table with Charlie, the cafe ghost. When Josie Jackson bought the business in June 1989, she too had no idea that the Paramount was haunted.

During the 1950s the cafe moved with the times, becoming the Paramount Milk Bar, but when Josie took over, she renamed it Knights Diner. It was just a couple of weeks after the family moved in, that Graham, her youngest son, complained one night that he could hear door handles rattling and someone moving about in the cafe downstairs. A quick check confirmed that all the doors and windows were securely locked and bolted. However, someone had made mischief there, because Josie found used coffee grounds and orange juice spilled across the cafe floor. This happened almost every night for the next two weeks. Then, small items such as tea towels would disappear, turning up again weeks later.

Just before Christmas that year, Josie and another son, Andrew, were working late baking batches of mince pies."I told him to go to bed at about 11.30pm and set about clearing up. It was while I was washing up at the sink that I started to feel something. The atmosphere changed. The kitchen was becoming colder and colder."

Putting it down to tiredness, Josie began to wash the flour from the table. And then it happened. There, in front of the cooker, not more than two feet away, was a man dressed in brown. He was staring at her.

"I ran out of the kitchen and started to climb the stairs but as I reached the third step I could go no further. Something was pulling me back. I could not move. It was like one of those awful dreams when you try to run but can't. I could feel hands clutching and gripping my arms, pulling me backwards."

Josie's screams brought Andrew running. "What's the matter mum?" he cried."You look as though you've seen a ghost". They searched the kitchen, which was now empty, and checked all the doors, which were locked and bolted. As Josie went up to her bedroom, Andrew came flying in. He had heard the kitchen door opening and footsteps walking across the tiled floor and up the stairs towards her.

"He was Always There..."

Since that night, Josie always sensed someone - or something - on that third stair. The lights at the top and bottom of the staircase would never stay on. Bulbs failed as soon as they were renewed, and she always kept a torch at the top and bottom of the stairs. "I just couldn't walk up and down there in the dark, and I always talked to myself on that staircase. I would not go up in silence. He was always there, waiting for me on the third stair."

With the help of Rosemary, a psychic, Josie discovered that her watcher on the stair is a ghost named Charlie, who worked in the building many years ago. His spirit told Rosemary he had been a 'bit violent' to women during his lifetime. He had once broken a woman's arm in the cafe and wanted to apologise. He had chosen Josie to make his peace with. Would she please listen to him?

Charlie's pleas however fell on deaf ears. "I just couldn't do it. I went cold all over when I knew he was there," said Josie.

After Rosemary's visit, Charlie moved more boldly about the place as though he was becoming more desperate. One night as she was having a drink with friends in the lounge, she felt an unseen hand push her arm so hard that she spilled her drink.

Once a butcher's shop and a wet fish shop, the cafe was built about 100 years ago on the old garden to Keats Cottage next door. The mother of the previous owner had also been pestered by 'something'. Perhaps she, too, had been unwilling to accept Charlie's apologies.

From that brief glimpse of Charlie in her kitchen, Josie said he was aged between 45 and 55, with dark hair and very piercing eyes. "I was caught like a rabbit in headlights, frozen to the spot by those eyes," she said with a shudder.

One September night in 1991, Josie returned home late to find Charlie asleep in a chair in the lounge. A friend who came in with her could also hear the sound of breathing, and they could both see a figure sprawled in the armchair.

"We walked over to the window making no noise, watching him all the time. But the moment we threw open the curtains, he vanished."

The cafe is The Paramount Restaurant now. Josie is there no longer. But what of Charlie, who waits for her on that third stair? Is his ghost bound in some way to the building, held prisoner by his own conscience until he can persuade a woman to accept his apology? Perhaps one day someone will agree to listen and grant forgiveness, delivering him from his weary penance.

THE HAUNTING OF HILLS

A phantom shopkeeper still counts his money at one of Ryde's oldest stores, while the ghost of an elderly customer continues to hunt for bargains. Hills of Ryde has prospered for a century in imposing Victorian premises in Ryde High Street. The site has been occupied for well over 300 years, first as an inn, The Nagg's Head, where once the author Henry Fielding took rooms. Later it was used by a blacksmith, baker, butcher, grocer and house agent, before becoming Hill and Co, drapers in the 1890s.

Tales of a ghost there had been whispered by staff over the years, but when Tony, an electrician for the Southern Electricity Board, was sent to the store to do a wiring job in 1962, he had no idea the shop was haunted.

Tony and his partner were busy in the front of the premises late one Thursday afternoon. It was early-closing day and apart from the two workmen, the shop was empty; the doors locked. Then came the sound of a bag full of money being tipped onto a glass-topped counter.

"It was a very odd, distinctive noise, and my mate walked over to the old cash-desk nearby to see what had caused it," said Tony." He came shooting back, his hair standing on end, and said there was absolutely nothing there. The old shop suddenly felt icy cold, and I rushed for the front door, forgetting it was locked."

The two electricians told themselves they had been imagining things, but half an hour later came the sound of a baby's rattle being shaken. In the nearby children's department they discovered a rattle lying on the counter. "That was it. We had had enough surprises for one afternoon. We unlocked the doors and were off," admitted Tony.

Manager of Hills since 1964, Mr Peter Jones still remembers the day one of his customers vanished - into thin air. So does Ray Harvey, now a postman and a local JP, who was working with Peter at the time. "She was a little elderly lady and she was wearing a long black coat and a black straw hat. Queer old-fashioned clothes they were," recalled Peter.

The strange little customer asked Peter for some pillows, and as he went off to fetch some, she disappeared. She had been the only customer in the store that lunch-time, but no-one ever saw her leave.

CHAPTER SEVEN

SOME VICTORIAN GHOSTS

THE HAUNTING HOUSEKEEPER

A Victorian ghost named Violet has appointed herself "keeper of the house" at Lower Knighton Farm, Newchurch, where her appearance is often preceded by a strong scent of the flower after which she was named.

Since the Newnham family moved there in 1984, they have grown accustomed to Violet popping up all over the house, and Mrs Angela Newnham often passes the time of day with her, calling out "Good morning, Violet", when she senses the shade has entered the room.

Angela, a registered healer, is psychic and has been developing her powers as a clairvoyant since childhood. She is often aware of Violet following her about the house, which was built in 1747 on the site of an earlier dwelling.

It was once occupied by the bailiff to nearby Knighton Gorges, visible from the old farm house, and sometimes on a very still night, the sound of a horse and carriage can be heard rumbling up the narrow winding lane. Angela has never been able to see the carriage, but late one night she heard the ghost horses neighing and snorting so clearly that she got up, convinced that her own horses were loose.

Angela and Gary, her builder husband, have renovated the old farmhouse as sympathetically as possible, restoring original features faithfully - which has evidently been acceptable to Violet.

Gary has encountered Violet only once and that happened when he was working alone in the house, opening up the old fireplace. The dining room suddenly went icy cold and he was so scared that when Angela came home, she found he had barricaded himself in their bedroom.

The dining room, with its 20 inch thick walls, central heating and large open fire, should be a warm room, but visitors constantly remark how cold it is. Angela simply explains that this is where Violet lives.

"All we really know about Violet is that she lived here during the 19th century when she was the housekeeper for Squire Carter and his family, and she feels she is still the 'keeper' of Lower Knighton Farm. I have never seen her clearly but just catch odd glimpses of her. She is always wearing a little muslin or lace bag of herbs and sweet-smelling perfume pinned to the bodice of her gown."

Violet is not a fan of loud pop music. Often when Angela and Gary's teenage daughter, Holly, is playing her radio or tapes at full volume, Violet steps in and switches them off. "I really don't blame her at all," confessed Angela. "Some of that music must sound pretty awful to a Victorian ear."

Apart from this aversion to loud noise and an irritating habit of moving small articles such as keys around the house, Violet is a benign ghost. "She is extremely kind and is trying to help me. We get on very well and it is often like having an invisible friend about the place."

These sentiments are shared by Mrs Ivy Welstead, of Newport Road, Lake, who although now in her seventies, can clearly recall Violet and her activities.

"I always knew when she was about as there would be a strong smell of parma violets in the room," said Ivy with a smile.

She and her family lived at the farm for 18 years, and during the last war they felt that Violet was somehow keeping them safe. "I saw her clearly on several occasions. She always wore a long, tight-waisted black dress with little black jet buttons down the front. She stood with her hands folded and her hair, medium brown I think, was rolled into a tight bun. She would look at me and smile."

Then, as now, Violet favoured the parlour and would often be standing in the corner of what is now the Newnhams' dining room, doing what she had always done during her life..... keeping the house.

THE PHANTOM MAID

When you don't believe in ghosts, it can be difficult to admit you have actually seen one - especially when you are a well-known Island hotelier and businessman. Mr Robin Thornton of Old Park Hotel, St Lawrence, found himself in exactly that situation a couple of years ago when the phantom of a young Victorian maidservant floated past him.

Robin, who has lived at Old Park for more than 40 years, was working in the oldest part of the building when "something" caught his eye. Glancing up, he saw, with total disbelief, a young serving girl wearing a long black and white striped Victorian dress, with a lace cap over her black hair.

"It was quite fascinating and I was not at all afraid. She did not appear solid. It was just like looking at a reflection in a plate glass window. She seemed quite friendly and just moved past me and disappeared," he recalled.

Robin has never seen her since, and both he and Shirley, his wife, have always found Old Park to be a warm and friendly place. Now an hotel, it was originally a farm house which was considerably enlarged in 1865 by its Victorian owner, German millionaire William Spindler

A local psychic has told them there is nothing evil there and certainly nothing to fear, but then, as Robin says, "Why should there be? There are no such things as ghosts!"

HOUSEPROUD SPECTRE

Occupants of a large rambling Victorian house in Terrace Road, Newport, must have had one of the neatest and most immaculate homes on the Island - thanks to their phantom housemaid.

When Norah and Horace Crutcher moved into the three-storey house opposite St John's Church, they were warned by a previous owner that the place was haunted by a ghostly maid who continued to sweep, dust and polish the place long after she was found lying dead at the foot of the cellar steps.

The house was divided into three flats and shortly after moving into one on the ground floor, Norah and Horace started to hear the chink of cups and plates being washed up in the empty flat above. Tea cloths would appear in the most unlikely places; pots and pans and cutlery would be moved in the night; while other tenants complained that the houseproud ghost was keeping them awake at night as she swept the staircase.

Twice, while they were sitting in their front room, the Crutchers heard the sound of brushing behind them and felt the draft of something dusting their chairs. Doors would open and close. Sometimes they would hear footsteps going down those cellar steps....but they never came up again.

THE GHOSTLY LOVERS

Over a century ago in Sandown, a young chambermaid threw herself off the pier killing herself and her unborn child. Once the pathetic story became known, her tormented lover followed the girl's example and, three days later, drowned himself by walking into the sea.

He was a married man, the master of a large fashionable villa in Leed Street, a respected member of local society, a lay preacher and organist at the nearby church. The scandal of the couple's affair and suicides rocked the seaside resort where, more than 100 years later, echoes of their poignant passion and despair were still touching the lives of others.

Their unhappy spirits continued to haunt that house, even after it became the Heathlands Hotel, where they were seen and heard by guests and staff. David Reid, whose family owned and ran the business in the 1970s, is now an estate agent in Sandown. He has vivid memories of his experiences at the old hotel, which has since been converted into holiday flats.

Within a few days of moving in, his mother felt a cat rubbing against her legs as she was standing at the kitchen sink, as if it wanted to be stroked or fed.

There was no cat at the hotel. What David's mother could feel was a ghost-cat demanding attention. After a few days she had had enough, and told it firmly to go away....which it did.

Many, many people saw and heard strange things in the hotel. Music would play softly in the empty lounge. One morning, David heard church music coming from the piano there. Thinking his father, a professional musician, was practising, he called out, "Hello, Dad", but there was no reply.

"As I walked in, the music stopped. The room was completely empty but the piano lid was up and the stool had been pushed back," David recalled. Baffled, he searched out his parents and found them in the kitchen, drinking coffee.

On another occasion, David himself was playing the piano, unaware that he had a ghostly audience sitting right behind him. The phantom was seen by one of the hotel guests, an elderly lady who had been reluctant to enter the lounge in case she disturbed David and his "friend" at the piano.

Her husband could see no-one there, but she described the apparition quite clearly. It was wearing a three-piece tweed suit with buttons, a gold hunter watch and chain. She said he had been lounging back in a chair immediately behind David, with his feet actually under the piano stool, and was clearly enjoying the music.

David's mother was often aware of presences in the hotel, especially in the bedrooms, and preferred to sleep in the newer annexe. David sometimes noticed cold spots in the old building, usually late at night in the hallway and on the staircase, and especially in the bedroom where, one summer's day, a 20th century chambermaid got the fright of her life when she came face to face with her 19th century counterpart.

She was changing the beds in one of the upstairs rooms, and returning with clean linen, found a young woman in a Victorian chambermaid's costume of long black dress and white apron standing by the bed. Thinking she was real, she asked the girl if she had come to help. In reply, the solid-seeming figure simply glided through the closed bedroom window...and vanished.

LACE TRIMMED PETTICOAT

Ghosts can turn up in the oddest, most unexpected, and occasionally very embarrassing places. Linzi Mathews would be the first to agree with this. A ghost appeared to her one day at work - when she was sitting on the loo!

The unforgettable incident happened in 1982 when Linzi, who worked for the DHSS at Broadlands House, Newport, went to the ladies' toilets on the first floor.

"I was sitting there, contemplating the floor, when I saw a foot appear at the bottom of the door. There was no gap there, the door went all the way to the floor. The foot was clad in a small, old-fashioned, pointed lady's shoe in dark grey, with buttons for decoration. Above the shoe I could see a line of lace, like the hem of a petticoat," said Linzi.

"It was as if the rest of the lady was standing on the other side of the door and she had just stepped forward. I didn't dare to open the cubicle door in case she really was there.

"I saw her foot for only a few seconds, then it vanished. I could still feel her presence, but when I did pluck up the courage to look, the room was completely empty."

The Ghost ate Buttered Toast

Linzi no longer works at Broadlands House, but said the Broadlands ghost had been seen, heard and smelt over the years. A strong smell of toasting bread would sometimes waft through the corridors, perhaps a faint remembrance of an afternoon tea party long ago.

Staff working in the upper part of the old house late in the afternoon sometimes hear footsteps echoing from empty rooms, the sound of knocking, and of furniture moving on the top landing.

Mr Derek Edge, estates manager, whose office is in the oldest part of the building where the toilets once stood, is half-hoping to glimpse something himself. Other staff have reported seeing the ghost of a young Victorian woman disappearing through walls. If Derek gets his wish, perhaps he will pay close attention to her shoes.

Although it has been extensively altered over the years, the old house still retains traces of its former glory, though now it is incorporated in the new DSS complex at Staplers Road.

Broadlands House was once the Island's lace factory which in its heyday employed almost 200 men plus winding boys and girls.

The factory was established in 1827 by Mr H.W. Nunn and Mr George Freeman, and was soon making enormous profits through selling French blonde lace. Queen Victoria and other ladies of the court were among the customers.

This silk blonde lace was as fine as a spider web and very costly, but sales were dependent on the fickle fashion industry. By 1870, old Mr Nunn decided to retire, but with no son to take on the business it was closed down, the machinery sold off, and many poor people found themselves out of work.

With the demise of the local lace industry, the old factory became Broadlands Home, a charitable establishment for poor spinsters and widow ladies who had fallen on hard times.

Established by Mrs Harvey of Shanklin, who inherited Broadlands after Mr Nunn's death, the charity also helped to train young working class girls as servants to be placed in service around the town. It is thought to have been one of these girls who was tragically killed in a fire at Broadlands Home around the turn of the century. It closed for good in the 1930s and was soon requisitioned by the Army at the start of the second world war for use by the Signal Corps, who sited a number of Nissen huts in the grounds. In 1949 it changed hands again, and was bought by the Ministry of Labour to house the National Assistance Board and Ministry of National Insurance.

So whose foot did Linzi Mathews see through the door and what are the origins of the Broadlands ghost who still enjoys her buttered toast of an afternoon? Was she one of the distressed gentlewomen fallen on hard times? No-one knows. But Linzi would be intrigued to find out if the petticoat she glimpsed was trimmed with some of that original Isle of Wight lace.

GHOST CHILDREN AND HAUNTED SCHOOLS

TRAGEDY AT NEWCHURCH

The 300-year-old schoolhouse at Newchurch has had many generations of village children through its doors. There, under the watchful eye of the resident schoolmaster, they learned to read; to write in copperplate script; and to do their sums. But by 1876 the old school was redundant. Supplanted by a larger elementary school, it became a private residence.

Ghosts still walk in the old school house. Tragedy has struck at least twice in its history, when the bodies of children have been found in an ancient stone-lined well nearby. Coroner's records for the year 1384 reveal that an inquest was held into the death of two-year-old Ellen Couherd who fell into a well at Langbridge and was found by her distraught mother, Juliana.

Centuries later the little stone schoolhouse was built nearby on land given by General Bocland, owner of Knighton Gorges. It consisted of 'a large school-room with a residence for the master and a garden, the whole number of scholars being about 30.'

A further tragedy cast a shadow over village life in 1747, when an inquest was held into the death of another child found in the Langbridge well. This time the verdict was murder. The man responsible was a relative of the young victim, Elizabeth Poell, who was about nine or ten years old. He was sent for trial at the Winchester Assize in the following year, where he paid for the foul deed with his own life.

The village Poor Book records that five shillings was spent in searching for the girl's strangled and battered body, and James Poell was 'carried to jail' at a cost of two pounds. Further details of the murder are lost in the mists of time, but it may well be that something of the little girl's shade still lingers in the old school, as does that of a dark-clothed man who has been seen and heard in one of the bedrooms and in the lane outside - close to the old well.

The former schoolhouse is now a charming pair of semi-detached cottages, Puckaster Cottage and Old School House Cottage. Until the late 1970's, Mrs Elizabeth Green lived there with her daughter Lizzie, who suffered from Down's Syndrome. Lizzie, locked into permanent childhood herself, spent many happy hours sitting in the garden on her swing or on the landing upstairs talking to her 'friend', a little girl no-one else could see. After Mrs Green died, Lizzie, then in her thirties, became a patient at Longford Hospital, Havenstreet.

Puckaster Cottage was bought by Frenchman Gilles Conrad and his family. After many months of work they moved in, but their dog, a large Scottish deerhound, refused to set foot - or paw - in the cottage. "One night we were so tired of this that four of us carried him inside and shut the door so he could not get out. He went wild. He was clearly so terrified that we let

Old School House Cottage, Newchurch. Home to a heavy breathing ghost.

Were the bodies of two young girls found in this well?

him out again," said Gilles.

Apart from the dog's decidedly odd behaviour, Gilles and his family had no other problems with the house. It was a warm and friendly place, as visitors confirmed, often remarking how relaxed they felt there. When the family sold up and moved out, it was with a feeling of regret.

However, in Old School House Cottage next door, things were rather different. It has been owned since 1964 by builder Mr Dave Cotton who has uncovered beams on which generations of Newchurch children have carved their names, initials and dates. He has found an old bread oven in the schoolhouse kitchen and discovered an old well outside near the kitchen door.

It was here that Judy Axford had a terrifying experience which she still vividly recalls, more than ten years later. Judy's story begins one winter's night in 1980, when she called on Dave.

The Dragging in the Darkness

He wasn't at home so she decided to wait, parking her little Hillman Imp in the lane by the cottage. As she sat in the dark, enjoying the stillness of the night, she heard from further down the lane in the marshland behind, a curious dragging sound.

"It was as if something heavy was being pulled along the ground. I peered into the darkness but could see nothing," she said. "As I sat waiting in my car the dragging sound came alongside, and stopped. I strained my ears. Then came a hoarse throaty gurgle. It was horrible. As if someone was being choked to death ..... or strangled.

"The image of stockings came into my mind. I was so terrified that I just started the car and shot off up the lane so fast that I almost blew up the engine. That sound was so loud, so inexplicable, my hair was standing on end. I really expected the car door to open. I couldn't get away fast enough."

It was several months later, after Judy had been living at the cottage for some time, that she had her next weird experience. "I always felt a presence and a coldness there, and had the feeling that I was never totally alone," she recalls.

It was at 10.30pm one October night that Judy was again witness to a chapter from the cottage's dark past. "I was reading in bed, when suddenly I looked up to find a figure standing by the bedroom window. I couldn't make out what clothes it was wearing, but it did have a large square-brimmed hat. It glided towards my bed, then disappeared. It was a strange eerie feeling, but I had half-been expecting something to happen, because there was always that sensation that something else was there with me," she said.

Judy turned back to her book and surprisingly fell asleep quite quickly. She was woken at 2am by the sound of rapid heavy breathing coming from the side of her bed where the figure had vanished earlier. "I held my own breath for a few seconds and listened. The room was freezing cold, and by this time I was very frightened indeed. I realised that whatever I had seen earlier had returned.

"I'll never know where I found the strength to get out of bed and turn the light on. I ran out onto the landing, switched on the light there, and made for the stairs to the attic where Dave was sleeping. Suddenly the landing light went out. It was like I was moving in slow motion; I tried to run up those narrow wooden stairs so quickly that I ended up on all fours. I burst into Dave's room and found him fast asleep."

Judy sobbed out her story trying to convince Dave that she had just seen a ghost in her room. "I grabbed his arm and would not let go. As Dave came downstairs with me, the landing light went on again. My bedroom felt like ice. It was full of chilled air, just as if someone had opened the door of a deep freeze. Then as we stood there, the light went out."

Judy never slept in that room again but insisted on sleeping downstairs on the settee in the lounge instead. "My old bedroom always felt cold after that night, and I always slept with the downstairs lights on. Often as I moved through the cottage, lights would switch themselves off after me."

As the old year ended, Judy had yet another brush with the supernatural at Old School House. Shortly after midnight on New Year's Eve, she went to the back door to call her cats in. "All of a sudden there was a tremendous clatter as a carriage or horse and cart rushed past me. I could hear the horses' hooves, their harness creaking and the sound of the wheels. But there was absolutely nothing there. It was very, very cold, but I had no sensation of air moving past. I was so shocked and terrified that I screamed. It was a scream from the very depths of my being. I frightened myself with the noise."

THE WROXALL SCHOOL PHANTOM

For more than 100 years, generations of Wroxall children learned their three R's at the little Victorian village school, but how many realised they were sharing their lessons with the school ghost?

The old school, which celebrated its centenary in 1973, was demolished 13 years later and its 100 pupils and staff moved into a purpose-built primary school nearby. New homes went up in place of classrooms and playgrounds, and since then, villagers who went to the old school have wondered what became of their ghost. Few were ever frightened; it was an accepted part of school life, and some youngsters even claimed to have seen the presence 'lurking' in the old toilet block.

Headteacher of Wroxall Primary School since 1980, Mike Davis, is convinced the old school was haunted. He heard footsteps in empty classrooms; furniture being moved late at night, and felt there was always a presence there.

"I was never alone in the place. Someone or something else was around. There were several cold spots which could be quite unpleasant, and I always disliked locking up at night in the dark. I would feel most uncomfortable and couldn't get out fast enough. Even my dog would not go into some parts of that school."

Elderly villagers believed the ghost was that of a workman who fell to his death from scaffolding when the school was being built, and Mike said that the presence always felt stronger in the infant and junior classroom and an upstairs room.

This feeling became overwhelming the day Mike decided to give the children a glimpse of the past with a Victorian Day. "They all came to school dressed in Victorian-style clothes. I dressed as their school master and we had an old-fashioned lesson complete with blackboard and slates.

"The atmosphere was most extraordinary and very powerful. The school that day felt quite weird, as if we had somehow evoked the past. I never tried it again."

School secretary Mrs Chris Mogg, who joined the staff in 1972, also heard those footsteps walking across an old wooden classroom floor when the building was locked and in darkness. "To me, the presence had an impish, almost mischievous feel, and it made me uneasy," she said.

"The old school was lovely during the day when it was filled with happy children. But when it was empty, it was a different place altogether, not a comfortable one.

"I am not at all sorry it was pulled down," Chris added quietly.

Demolished in 1986, old Wroxall Primary School was haunted by the ghost of a workman who was killed there more than a century ago.

MISS TRUTTLE'S SCHOOL

More than a century ago, a middle-aged spinster and teacher at Miss Truttle's School for Young Ladies in Brading is said to have committed suicide when a love affair went tragically wrong.

The old school is now a comfortable home for Sandown GP Lindi Reid and her family, and although a ghostly light from the long-dead teacher's candle was observed floating downstairs by the cottage's former owners, Lindi hasn't seen so much as a flicker since she moved in.

Situated at the bottom of Mall Road, the former schoolhouse, built during the seventeenth century, has a strangely tranquil atmosphere. Lindi may not notice anything untoward there, but her cats occasionally do. They will sometimes sit on the staircase, peering intently at something which no human eye can see.

A FIVE-GHOST FAMILY

An old school in Ryde is top of the class where ghosts are concerned. They wander freely around the old stone building, down corridors, up stairs and even through walls.

The Ferguson family who have made their home in the former school, now a pair of cottages in West Street, are amused by, and quite fond of their ghosts. Paul and Sandra Ferguson with children Thomas, Kerry and Fiona, bought their half of the property in 1978 shortly after moving to the Island. Within days, they noticed the delicious smell of baking bread wafting about the house at odd times. A welcoming and homely manifestation, this faded and finally stopped as soon as the family started renovating the cottage a few months later.

Over the years since then, no fewer than five ghosts have been seen by everyone except Sandra. "I would dearly love to see something," she said wistfully. "I feel quite left out. The only thing I have ever noticed here is the bread baking, and another very acrid smell which often precedes an appearance by one of the ghosts. "

There is no pattern to the ghosts' movements, and they are never seen together. Sometimes weeks can pass without one being spotted. They all seem quite solid, except for one elderly Victorian lady resembling Queen Victoria.

She wears a brown silken dress with starched petticoats which rustle as she glides through a wall at the top of the stairs into the cottage next door. This ghost has also been spotted taking a turn about the garden, but generally confines herself to the first floor landing, often putting in an appearance when the family is about to go out, or away on holiday. "We usually wave and say goodbye to her when we go out," Paul admitted. "Although she never acknowledges this or waves back."

Once a school for young ladies, the property later became a commercial hotel, run by a mother and her two daughters. However, emnity festered and as soon as the old lady died, the sisters lost no time in splitting it into two houses where they lived out their lives never speaking to each other.

The Fergusons have no idea why the house is so overcrowded with phantoms; for as well as the Brown Lady, the gallery of ghosts includes a young man in a grubby white shirt and dark trousers who stands rigid with fists so tightly clenched that the knuckles show white. He is sometimes seen in the basement bedroom and follows the line of a former passageway into the kitchen.

Then there is a rather scruffy spirit, wearing a dusty or chalky dark jacket rather like a morning coat. He too is perfectly harmless and wanders about just minding his own business.

Ghost Children

Two ghost children also live somewhere in the old school, and one, a little girl in a yellow dress, occasionally 'nips' round a corner in the dining room or lounge. "When our children were little they would sometimes rush into a room and lunge at something, trying to catch a ghost. They do seem to play with us, but really they are a very friendly lot, and do no harm. We are all so used to them that when we have visitors, we sometimes forget to warn them," laughed Paul.

Like the night Uncle Bob, an ex-Royal Navy diver, slept in that basement room. He was up early next morning demanding to know why he had not been told the house was haunted. He never slept there again.

A young student staying in that same room saw something but didn't actually mention the ghost - whether out of politeness or fear of ridicule, Paul and Sandra never discovered. "I went down there one morning to tidy up, and was amazed to find a row of crucifixes on the window-sill. Something was disturbing him there, but he never said a word to us about it," exclaimed Sandra.

The latest ghost, that of a little boy dressed in green, has been seen walking through the house to the garden, and sitting in a tree outside. Paul first saw him one warm summer evening, when Sandra and Fiona came home from Brownies and went out to the garden. Leading the way was what he took to be a young cub scout. "He was a jaunty little chap, and he was obviously chattering as he walked in front of Sandra and Fiona.

"When they came back indoors, I asked where the young lad was. They looked at me blankly. Then of course I realised....we had yet another ghost."

During their time at the cottage, many decidedly odd and inexplicable things have happened, but only a couple have been at all unpleasant. On one occasion, a tankard jumped or was pushed off the dining room dresser, hitting young Fiona on the head and cutting her badly. At this, the family gave warning that if anything violent happened again they would call in their vicar to get the place blessed.

Yet whatever is sharing their cottage seems to care about the family, for when Paul and Kerry have been ill in bed something has 'tucked' them in during the night. "It is a most peculiar feeling and it really is quite frightening. You actually feel a hand touching you, then the duvet or blanket is pulled up over you by something unseen," shuddered Paul

This happened several times when he was sleeping downstairs because of a bad back. At first, he thought Sandra had crept down to check on him. But it was no human hand that had touched him......

Meanwhile, in the adjoining cottage the lives of the Banks family have also been disturbed by the old school's resident ghosts - for whom walls are no barrier. They move around at will, treating the place just like home!

David and Carol with their two young daughters moved there in 1990. "The moment we opened the door it was welcoming and we knew we had to buy it," Carol said.

However, within a week she had smelt that acrid, burning odour that the Fergusons next door had also noticed. Their three-year-old complained of seeing a 'wobbly witch' coming out of the wall on the landing, and said she was wearing a dark dress and had 'horrible red lips'.

"At the time we knew nothing about the ghosts next door, and just thought Jenny was imagining things. The name 'wobbly witch' had come from a Rupert Bear book we had been reading to her, with pictures of an ugly old woman, which had obviously stuck in her mind."

After this, Jenny often told her mother she had seen the 'wobbly witch' on the landing and in her bedroom. One day when she was in Carol's bed, the little girl announced, "Mummy, the wobbly witch is standing right next to you. She has got really red lips and she is really horrible."

"I could see nothing, but I shot away from that wall immediately," Carol said with a shudder.

Seven-year-old Sarah also encountered one of the cottage spirits but was quite unperturbed by it. A large stone she found on the beach had been left on top of a cupboard in the hall, together with a glass pebble. One afternoon as Sarah watched in amazement, her stone started to rock violently and the glass pebble flew towards her, landing gently at her feet. The little girl rushed in to tell Carol, "Mummy, I think we have got a ghost and it's playing with me."

Twice since then, if Sarah has been upset or in a temper, a ghostly light has appeared to her which the little girl describes as 'a white light floating thing'. Like Sandra next door, Carol has never seen any of the cottages' ghosts herself, but she believes they mean her family no harm. "This is a light and happy home. Children are never frightened here. I see no reason why we can't all live together - after all, the ghosts were here long before we moved in."

CHAPTER NINE

HAUNTED MANORS

THE LAUGHING GHOST

Historic Haseley Manor at Arreton is the sort of place where you would expect to find a ghost. According to owner, Ray Young, at least three have surprised some of the thousands of visitors who come to Haseley every year.

Ray, a former Mayor of Brading, whose family has lived on the Island for generations, bought the manor in 1976 and has invested almost £1 million restoring it. Listed in the Domesday Book, Haseley is part mediaeval with various additions by its Tudor, Stuart, Georgian and Victorian owners. It has been home to Sir Edward Horsey, a Captain and Governor of the Island. From 1609 until 1951, the manor belonged to the Fleming family, ending its days in ignom+iny and a certain squalor after it had been converted into farm labourers' dwellings. Since Ray and his family moved there, Haseley Manor has started to live again, as have the ghosts - which once enjoyed a mortal existence within its walls.

There is nothing frightening about the manor's ghosts. One has a pathetic and unhappy history but another, that of a handsome young gentleman, is positively brimming with good humour and is always laughing. He has been seen on several occasions, and one visitor, Charles Stewarts-Warwick, was able to draw an accurate sketch of the laughing ghost which now hangs in the manor. This portrays him wearing knickerbocker trousers and a white shirt-like blouse, belt, leather boots and a black wide-brimmed hat.

To Mr Stewarts-Warwick, the young ghost seemed 'terribly jolly'. "He threw back his head with silent laughter and I could actually see some of his blackened teeth. He gave me quite a surprise," the visitor told Ray.

Another holidaymaker was able to add to this description a few years later, when she too met the laughing ghost. "He had a beard, a moustache and wore a sword belt about his waist," said the startled woman.

One summer afternoon in 1991, a group of ladies came into the house praising the authenticity and attention to detail of its restoration. They were especially taken with the group of monks fishing in one of the old pools in the manor grounds. "What they didn't realise was that the monks were nothing to do with us. They were visitants from a time long ago when the house was owned by Quarr Abbey, and the ponds, or stewes, were stocked with fish by the monks," Ray explained.

An Echo of Despair.....

Ray has never seen any of "his" ghosts, which disappoints him, for he would love to meet one and question it about Haseley's history. "Some people go into the house and beat a hasty retreat because they sense something not quite right. Others have actually felt an unhappy presence there," Ray said.

This must be Haseley's tragic young ghost, Amelia, who hanged herself

Haseley Manor, near Arreton, home to a gallery of ghosts.

in an attic room in 1843. Her body was discovered by her fellow servants and given a hasty burial in an unmarked grave on unconsecrated ground.

Amelia was considered the belle of the district and courted by many local lads. Although a servant, she came from a good family - whose descendants still live in the area - and young Amelia lost her heart to a farmer's son.

He, it seems, took advantage of her, then cast her aside to marry another. Distraught, disgraced and pregnant, poor Amelia told the other servants: "This is my last day's work at Haseley." Then went alone to the attic room to commit suicide.

With no signs of grief, her former beau went through with his wedding as Amelia was being buried the very next day. Self-destruction was a mortal sin, and an echo of Amelia's despair lingers in those attic rooms.

It has been felt by a number of visitors to Haseley, including a local psychic who has also made contact with the melancholy spirit of a long-dead squire's daughter there.

A member of the Fleming family, this girl also loved unwisely and with unhappy consequences, said the psychic. She fell in love with a boy from a poor family and when her father found out, she was forbidden to have anything to do with him. They continued to gaze at each other every Sunday in church, and one day, unable to bear their separation, met once more.

Scarred for Life

When he discovered her disobedience, Squire Fleming whipped his daughter so savagely that she was scarred for life. From then on, she always wore long-sleeved dresses to hide the livid marks on her arms and body. The punishment also left her with mental scars which never healed until she died, a bitter and unhappy woman. Her spirit has not found peace and still haunts the home where she lived out her days.

Ray had his doubts about this story until a visitor told him that her ancestors had once lived at Haseley. Although not a member of the direct Fleming line, she said her many-times-great-grandmother had been disowned by the family. Married against her will, she ended her days at the manor as the wife of a tenant farmer while the Flemings moved to a grander estate at Binstead.

This mournful ghost was seen recently by Angela Newnham of Newchurch, when she was working at the manor. "I was walking in the house and I felt drawn to the window overlooking the gardens near the stream," she explained.

"Looking out, I saw the ghost of a lady walking in the sunshine. She was wearing a turquoise day-dress with a bustle. A long-sleeved dress, it had fancy pointed cuffs that completely hid her arms and hands. Aged about thirty, she wore her light brown hair piled up on top of her head," said Angela.

These shades from the manor's chequered history never worry Ray or his visitors. They move about the manor on their ghostly business keeping themselves very much to themselves. Although he has never seen one himself, Ray is secretly pleased that Haseley is haunted. Many manors have ghosts and it is fitting that such a fine old house should have its share.

SOBBING IN THE ATTIC

When the Pinder family became the new owners of Pidford Manor they didn't realise that, along with one of the Island's most historic and charming houses, they would also be taking on the resident ghosts.

The house can just be glimpsed from the main Rookley road, standing in acres of parkland. Although it is considered one of the Island's minor manors, there has been a house at Pidford since 1301. A subsequent manor house was occupied by Sir James Worsley, a page to King Henry VII, and in 1840 the rebuilt Pidford Manor became the residence of authoress Elizabeth Sewell, who wrote many of her 57 books there.

Mrs Sheila Pinder was alone in the house one night when she heard loud and angry crying coming from one of the old attic nurseries. It was so real that she raced upstairs. But as she reached the landing the noise stopped abruptly.

"It was definitely a child or young person sobbing uncontrollably in a hurt and angry way. It made me very uneasy," Sheila admitted. Later, she heard from the manor's previous owners that the ghost of a child had been both seen and heard in the same part of the house.

One woman, who lived at Pidford for eleven years, often sensed a young child standing by her bed in the night. Once, the feeling was so strong that she hurried upstairs to the attic bedrooms to check on her own sleeping daughters. Climbing the stairs she saw a little child's hand going up the staircase too. Only the hand was visible, and it was at the wrong level. The family learned later that the old attic stairs had been moved from their original position.

"I never saw anything else", said the former lady of the manor. "I felt it was a young girl and she was unhappy. My children would sometimes hear footsteps and creaking of floorboards on the landing between their attic rooms, but after we had been there a while the feeling disappeared. The house was full of children and laughter and I don't think the little ghost was lonely any longer."

Pidford's other ghost is a rather corpulent elderly gentleman in his night attire. Sheila saw him standing in front of her bedroom window early one morning. He was wearing an oriental brocade dressing gown, patterned in rich dark colours of crimson and gold, and he had an odd little nightcap on his head. "He seemed to be looking straight at me and I was really quite frightened. I decided to leave him to it and went downstairs to make myself a cup of coffee. When I returned, the bedroom was empty."

As a Roman Catholic, Sheila invited her local priest to bless the house shortly after the family moved in. "He asked me if I had seen any ghosts there. I thought this was rather a strange question for a priest. Now I think I know why," she said.

A HANDFUL OF TINY BONES

A baby's continual crying so distressed the nanny at a Seaview home that she left her job. Nothing she did could comfort the infant - it was a ghost.

Although this happened more than forty years ago, Ted Jones of Ryde, is still haunted by the pathetic little tale. He was just a lad of 16 when it happened, working as a painter with a local firm, renovating a large eighteenth century house in Oakhill Road.

The nanny had left, it was said, because of the ghostly crying and the sound of running water which were always heard together. A local clergyman was asked to bless the house to rid it of the unwanted presence. "It didn't work," said Ted. The crying continued until a plumber came to check and renew the pipes. Up in the roof, directly over the room where the sounds were heard, he found an ancient lead-lined water tank. It was bone dry and full of the dust of many years. It also contained some fragile little bones. A tiny child's bones. The tank was removed, and from that day onwards the crying was never heard again.

CHAPTER TEN

ANIMALS AS GHOSTS

THE CAT WHO CAME BACK

Tiddles the cat was a placid affectionate black and white mog, who lived out most of her 19 years in a house at Bedworth Place, Ryde. She would spend most of the day asleep in her favourite armchair, or sunning herself on the window-sill, and when she wanted to go out, she would signal her intentions by scratching loudly on a piece of chipboard by the kitchen door.

Her owners Chris and Bob Footer, and their children Stewart and Anita, who had grown up with Tiddles, mourned her passing, for she was a loved member of their family. The old cat actually died in her favourite armchair in Anita's arms.

After a decent interval, the Footers acquired two more cats, Brandy and Hobie, although of course they could never replace Tiddles. Which is just as well because she has recently come back .....as a ghost.

"We just couldn't believe it at first," Stewart said. "She came back in November 1991, about a year after her death. I heard her scratching at my bedroom door to be let in, the way she had always done. But when I opened the door, there was nothing there."

Stranger still, when one of the family is sitting in Tiddles' old armchair, they occasionally feel an invisible cat jump up and sit on their lap. "It always happens in that chair, and she will tread on my feet before jumping up, the way she always did when she was alive. I have felt her kneading my leg with her paws before curling up, then there is the sensation of a heavy little body on my lap," Stewart explained.

This lasts up to 45 seconds, then suddenly the weight is gone. Stewart and his family have even seen a cushion on the chair being compressed by the weight of the unseen cat but he cannot bring himself to put his hand down to stroke her ghost - afraid perhaps of what he might feel.

Out in the kitchen, Tiddles continues to weave around their ankles as if asking to be fed, rubbing her ghostly little body against Chris's legs when she stands at the sink. The sound of claws scratching the board by the kitchen door is still heard - not only by human ears, but by Brandy and Hobie as well.

"One night I heard Tiddles' old signal, and there in the kitchen, just staring at the sound was Hobie with his eyes almost popping out of his head and his fur standing on end," said Stewart. "Both he and Brandy sense Tiddles is still around and I believe they actually see her sometimes, especially in her old chair, as they will walk up to it, stare intently at the cushion for a few seconds and then back away.

"I would give anything to know why Tiddles has come back to us. We all loved her and she was happy here. Perhaps animals do have souls after all. I just wish we could actually see her as well.....and hear her purr again. She is a very special cat."

CAT IN A BASKET

Kay Liggens, of Copse Lane at Freshwater, was emptying her laundry basket one day when she had the fright of her life. For there, curled up asleep on a pile of clothes was Titch, her black cat, who had been put down by the vet a few weeks before. "I lifted the lid and there she was, looking quite solid and real. Then she just vanished. I was really quite shaken," Kay exclaimed.

Titch has turned up twice more in the middle bedroom where Kay has found her little ghost lying asleep on the carpet. And once Titch actually got up, stretched herself and started walking towards her former mistress before vanishing into thin air.

THE CAT WHO FLOATED

Whiskers the black cat wasn't feeling particularly lucky the day he began to levitate. In the words of his owner, David Taylor, he was off "like a bat out of hell" as soon as his paws touched solid ground again. David and his former wife, Barbara, were at home in Pan Estate, Newport, watching television when it happened. Whiskers was fast asleep on a chair near the set.

"Out of the corner of my eye I saw something move, and as I turned I saw the cat float slowly up into the air. I nudged my wife and, while we watched, Whiskers went on rising towards the ceiling. When he reached a height of about seven feet, all of a sudden he woke up, saw where he was, panicked, and dropped like a stone to the floor.

"When he touched down, he flew round and round the room, until we let him out. It was very odd, but it was even more strange that neither of us mentioned what had just happened, although we had both witnessed it. We sat there for several minutes in silence. Finally I said,'Did you see something strange happen?' My wife confirmed that she too had watched the cat floating above our heads, and that was that."

Whiskers did not seem any the worse for his sudden rise when he came back indoors later in the day. The chair on which he had been snoozing had been acquired second-hand, and shortly after this incident Barbara moved it upstairs to the bedroom.

There it continued to exert a strange influence. Whiskers refused to go near the chair again, but one night when Barbara went into the bedroom she saw something lying there. It looked like big black furry animal, but as she moved closer the creature vanished.

David doesn't know where that chair is now, but if you have recently bought an old chair and think there may be something odd about it......you and your cat had better beware.

THE PURITAN'S DOG

When Jack and Paddi Eales took on the job of renovating an eighteenth century stone cottage at Thorley, near Yarmouth, they didn't count on their resident ghost showing such an interest in the work.

They bought Newhouse Cottage in 1969 and over the next ten years did their best to overcome the years of neglect it had suffered; delighting in opening up fireplaces and exposing timbers and beams. As they worked, Jack and Paddi, who are both professional entertainers, became aware that "something" was watching them.

"We never actually saw it, but it would be there whenever we were doing anything major to the old cottage. The place has a friendly benign feeling, and whatever is here was very curious and interested in the work. I feel it could be a dog because it seems to be close to the ground. It often sits in a corner behind my chair in the rear sitting room - although we have found it in other rooms where we have been working," Jack said.

Built in 1762, Newhouse Cottage almost certainly replaced a much earlier house; an old stone well in the garden dates from the thirteenth century. Now filled with rubble, it serves as a very damp but desirable abode for an elderly resident toad.

Here by the old well, late one summer afternoon, Jack caught a glimpse of a man who had been dead for at least three hundred years. Dressed in black Puritan garb with a high tapering hat, coat with white at the neck, calf-length breeches with white stockings, and black shoes with shiny buckles, he appeared to be walking from the cottage towards the well.

For a brief moment he seemed real and solid, but then that echo from the cottage's past "winked-out" and Jack was left standing alone again, with only the timeless chirping of crickets and lazy humming of bees for company.

THE DOG'S REVENGE

A little ginger and white Cavalier King Charles spaniel was once the treasured and cosseted pet of a young girl, remembered today only as the Blue Lady of Nettlestone. But two centuries ago, the pair lived and played at Nettlestone Priory, which stands on the site of a mediaeval building.

A portrait of the young girl once hung in the dining room. In it, she wore a blue dress trimmed with silver lace; on her wrist perched a canary held by a satin ribbon; at her feet frisked the little dog.

She appeared to be about fourteen years old, and sadly she died shortly after her portrait was painted. Her pet spaniel was later stuffed and today lies in a glass case on a window ledge at The Priory (a more detailed account of their story appears in "Ghosts of the Isle of Wight".) The Blue Lady however continued to love this pet dog from her lonely grave.

In 1927 when the Priory was sold, its furniture and contents were dispersed. The little spaniel was bought by a curio dealer. The Blue Lady's spirit was distraught; her shade was seen running about the house, sobbing and calling for her lost pet. Servants began to give in their notice.

The new owner, an American asked why they were leaving. As soon as she heard, the woman started an Island-wide search for the little dog, finally tracking him down to an antique shop in Newport. Purchasing him for £1, she bore the creature home in triumph and from that day on, all was peaceful again.

Since then, successive owners of The Priory have made sure the little dog is not disturbed, and although the young girl's ghost has recently been seen, she appeared to be quite happy. Her shade was spotted in the lounge of what is now the Priory Hotel one evening by Roy, a retired gardener. He mistook the ghost-child for a guest and chided her that it was long past her bed-time. In reply, the girl in the long blue dress simply vanished.

Other ghosts still walk there and a pair of monks have been seen gliding about the grounds. One visitor even complained that a phantom knight in full armour had appeared in her room one night.

One foolish former member of staff at The Priory scoffed at tales of ghosts and hauntings. He laughed when he heard the story of the Blue Lady and her dog. He took the little spaniel from its resting place to play practical jokes on fellow members of staff, and one night he even put it in someone's bed.

But he won't touch the dog now; he doesn't go anywhere near it....not since the day it walked across his bedroom floor right in front of him.

While pressing a clean jacket for a wedding reception at the hotel that afternoon, he heard the sound of a dog's paws on the carpet. There, walking across the floor towards him, was the ghost of a little Cavalier King Charles spaniel. The room went icy cold, the ghost-dog passed him without a second glance and vanished.

"I am convinced the dog was exacting some sort of revenge, punishing me for what I had done and for laughing at its story," he said, very chastened. "I know better now and there is no way I will ever touch him again."

Curious guests can still see the little dog in his glass case, looking a trifle weary now after two centuries. But does his spirit still frolic with that of the mistress he adored, somewhere beyond the grave ? Perhaps.......

The Priory Hotel, home of the Blue Lady of Nettlestone and the little dog she loved from beyond the grave.

63

CHAPTER ELEVEN

POLTERGEISTS AND THEIR TRICKS

There seems no end to the tricks poltergeists play. Noisy, mischievous, spiteful and unpredictable, they behave rather like hyper-active but invisible children and can make life very unpleasant for the victims of their pranks.

Poltergeist, a German word, means noisy ghost or racketing spirit and their activities have been recorded for thousands of years. Modern day poltergeists like to open doors and windows; switch on lights and electrical equipment; turn on taps; move furniture about and rearrange ornaments.

They can make objects disappear only to materialise somewhere completely different and often have a fascination for money and jewellery. Their behaviour is pointless, aimless. No country is free of them and poltergeist activity was recorded as long ago as 858 BC.

But what is a poltergeist? A link between its activity and the presence in a household of an adolescent boy or girl, who is thought to be a source of unconscious emotional energy or 'psychic hormones', is often made. Yet in many poltergeist cases no such youngster is involved. Here are just a few stories of Island poltergeists.....

THE JEALOUS LITTLE GHOST

A spiteful and jealous little ghost did everything it could to make young Charlotte Ridley's life a misery. It would try to hurt her, pull her hair, make her cry and break her toys.

Charlotte's worried mother could only watch helplessly. An appeal to their local priest was made in vain. He refused to exorcise the family's cottage at Middleton, Freshwater. Eventually Bruce, Charlotte's elder brother, decided to act, and with holy water and a book on the supernatural he performed his own ritual cleansing, a sort of do-it-yourself exorcism which seemed to work.

The Ridley family bought Millbank, a 300-year-old former chapel, from a religious organisation in 1977. The old stone cottage had also once served as a barn, a forge and a carriage repair shop, as well as being a farm house.

Mrs Niki Ridley often wonders if the former owners who sold them the chapel knew there was "something" wrong with it, for after moving in, the family discovered coins, halfpennies and farthings, had been carefully placed on every window-sill in the house. An old superstition advises that this be done to keep the Devil out.

The first odd thing the Ridleys noticed was the shade of an elderly hunch-backed man which would shoot across the upstairs landing in front of them. "We would always duck because he had his arm raised and we got the impression he was going to fly straight into us, but although there was never any physical contact, we always suffered a splitting headache after an encounter with him," said Niki.

It was not until Charlotte was born that the little ghost's jealous antics began. When she was about ten months old and sitting in her rocker chair on the kitchen table, baby and chair were suddenly catapulted right across the room. Charlotte banged her head on the washing machine and spent a night in hospital with concussion.

After that Niki would not let her tiny daughter out of her sight. "If I went out of the room, she would start to scream. Quite often I would see her hair being tugged quite hard by invisible hands. All sorts of nasty things would happen to her toys and anything of hers. I am convinced it was a poltergeist, and a spiteful one at that."

The Uninvited Party Ghost

Only once was the poltergeist ever seen, when it made an uninvited appearance at Charlotte's birthday party. A little girl wearing a red dress raced past Bruce, who was keeping count of the toddlers, went upstairs - and vanished.

"Perhaps she thought it was safe to materialise with so many other children about," said Niki. "Or maybe she was lonely and just wanted to join in and play."

Soon after this, Charlotte started to wake in the middle of the night. She always slept in Niki's bed where her mother could keep an eye, and a hand, on her. The baby would be wide awake, laughing and babbling at something unseen.

One night Charlotte became very excited. Niki could sense a presence in the room with them. She began to feel afraid. "It was frightening and rather sinister. Something evil was there with us and we had to get rid of it, using bell, book and candle if necessary. Our parish priest would not come and cleanse the house, so my son decided to attempt it himself with prayers and holy water. Thankfully it worked. He sprinkled that water all over the place and it even got rid of the old man on the top landing. The whole house felt clean and good again."

The cottage stood empty for six years when the family moved to Africa, where Niki's husband David ran a railway for a mining company. When they returned in 1989 she was conscious of a tranquil atmosphere, as though someone had been caring for Millbank while they were away.

"There is still something here watching over us. Doors open and close, and you can put something down and it will be moved. It really can be most infuriating, but now it is not malicious, just mischievous," smiled Niki gratefully.

THE GHOST WHO LIKED CHOCOLATE CAKE

Whatever haunts the Clarendon Hotel and Wight Mouse Inn at Chale has an impish sense of humour and a fondness for ham sandwiches and chocolate cake.

Jean and John Bradshaw have run the Clarendon, originally a 17th century coaching inn, since 1979, and in that time they have built it into one of the Island's finest hostelries which was awarded the Egon Ronay Family Pub of the Year accolade.

Previous owners Pat and Norman Stagg did warn the Bradshaws that an old sailor haunted the place, adding that his bent and bearded figure had been seen on the top landing. "We didn't really take them seriously," said Jean. "But after we moved in, we knew there definitely was something here."

At that time, only Jean and John and their two children, James and Sally, lived on the premises. "I would wake at about 6.30am to get the children ready for school and start preparing the bar food. John would usually sleep in if he had been working late. This particular morning was no different."

While the children were having their cereal, Jean packed James's lunch-box with a ham sandwich, slice of chocolate cake, apple and crisps, and put it out for him on the worktop. The school bus arrived and James, ready to leave, asked Jean for his packed-lunch. But he never took it to school that day. It had vanished. James went off empty-handed, and later that morning Jean had to drive to Ventnor with more sandwiches and cake for him.

"I was furious. I knew I had made his lunch that day and put it ready. I hadn't even left the kitchen. It was a complete mystery but the fact was, it had disappeared."

Two months later, Jean decided to clear out several huge chest freezers full of cooked food which she had inherited from Pat. The locked freezers were in a locked utility room outside, and Jean had never opened them.

"I started to empty the stuff out. There, at the very bottom of a freezer, buried under mountains of food, was the missing lunch-box. I couldn't believe my eyes. Everything was still in it and frozen solid. "How it got there is a complete and utter mystery to this day. We all laugh about it now, but it was rather frightening at the time."

As the family settled down in their new home they grew accustomed to things going missing. Keys would disappear almost as soon as they were put down, said Jean. Ornaments were moved, and sometimes in the morning she would come downstairs to find furniture had been changed around during the night.

One evening the pub's Christmas Club record book completely disappeared. John and Jean hunted high and low. They almost took the place apart as it was the only copy they had.

Next morning the book was back again, in the very drawer it was always kept in. Jean doesn't know where it went, but she has a pretty shrewd suspicion that their pub spirit might know something.

"He isn't malicious, just friendly and mischievous. We haven't heard from him in quite a while now - not since the business took off and became really busy. Perhaps it's all too much for him and he has moved on to find somewhere quieter where his pranks will be appreciated," Jean said.

A SMASHING TIME...

A naughty poltergeist had a smashing time at a large old house in Elmfield, Ryde, at the expense of Mrs Janet Eldridge, her husband Des, and their daughter Lorraine. Glasses would shatter and break, a Pyrex cup exploded and reinforced windows shook so hard that they cracked in two.

The family would also hear the mutter of voices in animated conversation coming from empty rooms, although they could never quite make out what was being said as the noise would stop immediately if the door was opened.

The problems with glass started one morning when Janet found a Pyrex bowl full of water and plant cuttings had split during the night. The next thing to go was an empty glass cup sitting on a kitchen table, which suddenly, and for no apparent reason, exploded.

Then, as Janet was out in the garden, a thick reinforced window in her shed split in two with an almighty crack and the top section fell out, narrowly missing her foot. Back indoors, she discovered a thick sheet of glass from the centre of the coffee table had been lifted out and placed, undamaged, on the floor, with the potted plant from the table on the floor next to it.

"I was fed up with it all by this time. Speaking into thin air I said, half in jest, 'If you must break things - will you please stick to plastic'."

This message was received and understood for next morning, as Janet was cleaning her teeth, her toothbrush fell into two pieces......it was made of plastic.

"This thing obviously had a sense of humour," Janet decided. After a short foray into plastic, it turned its attentions back to glass. As she was sitting in the kitchen drinking tea one afternoon, the windows started to shake and vibrate violently and there was a heavy thumping on the glass. "This was the last straw. I had had enough. I told whatever it was that glass was dangerous.

"If you want to be here you are welcome to stay, but we have got to come to terms. Unless you can behave, I will have to get you removed," she warned.

On a more conciliatory note, Janet added, "This is my home and I am staying here, but there is plenty of room for both of us."

Ghost on the Telephone

After this little chat, things seemed to settle down. There were no more problems with glass. Instead the poltergeist turned its mischievous attentions to the telephone. Every time someone came to the house to talk to Janet, the phone would ring but there was never anyone at the other end. She had the lines checked on several occasions, but there was nothing wrong, just a jealous little spirit which did not like Janet paying attention to other people.

During the years she lived at the house, she never saw her poltergeist, but husband Des and their friend Jill did one day, although neither of them believed in ghosts. They both saw and described in detail the little girl, dressed all in white, whom they saw falling backwards off the high stone garden wall. When Janet and Lorraine arrived home that morning, they encountered the panicking pair running down the drive. The image had been so real that Des and Jill thought it was Lorraine, then aged nine, who had fallen from the wall.

"We hunted high and low, but there was no child, and there never had been. I believe it was our little ghost playing tricks again. She had been sitting on top of the wall and just tipped over backwards and disappeared," Janet said.

After this she tried to find out if a child had ever died in the grounds...and yes, she discovered that many years ago a baby had been buried nearby, a little premature scrap of a thing. Miscarried and stillborn, the tiny girl was buried by her father. She had been wrapped in white.

THE MAGPIE POLTERGEIST

Whatever shares Veniscombe House, Newchurch, with owners Ian and Sue Debrett seems to have a magpie-like fascination for shiny gold objects and jewellery. They always turn up again eventually, sometimes years after they disappeared. Their ghost is no thief, he simply likes to borrow things.

The old house dates back in part to the 14th century, although over the years, owners have made many alterations. Despite its great age, Veniscombe has a warm and welcoming feel, and years ago the annual church fetes were held in its gardens.

After almost 30 years at Veniscombe, Sue has never yet seen the ghost although she has heard it countless times. Both she and Ian have grown used to the three sharp, urgent raps on the front door which can happen any time of the day or night. Sue has often heard footsteps on the landings when the house is empty, and when her children were young she would often run upstairs ready to tell them to get back to bed, only to find them fast asleep. Whatever had been scurrying around upstairs, it wasn't her children.

"Sometimes I would be standing in the kitchen and feel tiny hands plucking at my skirt at toddler level, but there was never anything there. We just learned to accept such things. There is nothing frightening here, it is actually rather nice," said Sue.

That is not what Ian said when he discovered the ghost had turned off their washing machine and enormous chest freezer. This has happened more than once, and as Ian has since found out, it is impossible for the switches to have been knocked accidentally.

"It was a deliberate act and happened twice as I actually walked into the room. That freezer weighs a ton and you have to pull it out from the wall to reach the switches," said Ian.

He is certain that whatever haunts Veniscombe is male, and interestingly, an entry in the Newchurch Coroner's Roll for 1377 shows that a John Grontale was killed with a knife during a struggle in a field called Fenycombe (Veniscombe). Does his earthbound spirit remain there? Both Ian and Sue sometimes wonder.

It is only their ghost's light-fingered tendencies that cause annoyance. Sue once lost a favourite gold medallion and after searching high and low thought it had gone for good. However, five years later when carpets were being taken up during redecoration, the medallion was found in the middle of the bedroom floor....under a heavy carpet.

A new belt of Ian's, with a gold buckle, was lost for several weeks. This reappeared coiled in the middle of the very chair from which it had vanished. Sue has recently lost her favourite gold earrings, heavy and ornate, a present from Ian. She is sure they have only been 'borrowed' and will turn up again...one day.

PHANTOM WITH A FILOFAX

A ghost staying at the Holmes Court Hotel, Colwell Bay, has a sense of humour and a head for figures. It loves to purloin cheque books, address and account books, keys, and anything to do with money and numbers.

It positively delights in setting off the hotel's automatic fire alarm in the dead of night, and in sending clocks haywire. But owners Barry and Anne Hopwood and their children are quite used to the ghost's pranks by now and have learned to take them in the right spirit.

Barry, a former racing driver, and his family have built the hotel into a recognised centre for watersports and other outdoor activities, and their guests come from far and wide. They too are not immune from the ghost's attentions and several have "lost" things there.

The first Barry knew of their friendly phantom was when two valuable oil paintings flew several feet across a room and landed face down by the window. Sheila, a member of staff, was washing up in the kitchen when she heard someone whispering close behind her, but when she turned, the room was empty.

Then the clocks began to go crazy and would start and stop, gain and lose hours, for no reason. When the Hopwoods mentioned this to the former owner, she just laughed and said it had happened to her too.

Members of the New Seekers pop group stayed at Holmes Court one summer, and as they were booking their next visit, one of the group went to fetch a business card from his car outside. He came in, white and shaken, with a Filofax in his hand. The designer diary was icy cold, although the temperature in the car was well over 80 degrees that day.

He told Barry and Anne that the Filofax had been missing for months, and he had just found it sitting in the middle of the driver's seat in his car.

When the musicians returned that winter, another extraordinary thing happened. As they were settling the bill, a cheque book vanished from one of the group's back trouser pocket - only to turn up after a lengthy search, in the pocket of a jacket he had never worn, zipped inside a suit holder out in the car.

Then one of Barry's account books disappeared from a desk. He combed the hotel from top to bottom and this time the missing article turned up beneath the centre of a heavy mattress.

No-one has ever seen the hotel ghost, although Barry and Anne often glimpse shadows on the staircase, hovering around the first three steps. Barry has also noticed a ghostly figure standing outside the front door. "We have learned to live with it and accept its little eccentricities. There is a lovely warm and friendly feel to the hotel which guests notice. I think the ghost must like us, for if we ever talk of selling the hotel, it becomes agitated and then we have trouble with the clocks and lights - and of course the fire alarm."

CHAPTER TWELVE

NEW HOUSES HAVE GHOSTS TOO

A house doesn't have to be old or historic to have a ghost. Many of the hauntings in this chapter occur in newly-built homes...

HAUNTED COUNCIL HOUSE

When Judy Axford and her son Darren, then aged nine, moved into their newly-built house, owned by Medina Borough Council and overlooking Wootton Creek, they never dreamt it came complete with a ghost.

Psychic ability and a sensitivity to the supernatural obviously run in Judy's family (another of her experiences is told elsewhere in this book) but the two-bedroom house in Mary Rose Avenue looked and felt normal. Then, one evening at about 9pm, when Judy and Darren were sitting in the lounge watching television, she glanced up to see the figure of a tall man appear in the fireplace and walk across the room....right through the chairs.

Not wanting to frighten her son, she suppressed any exclamation of surprise, but Darren had seen it too. "He was sitting there with his mouth wide open looking as if he had seen a ghost.. which of course he had."

The boy asked, "Did you see that, mum? It was a man wasn't it?" The figure, which appeared quite solid, was very tall but moved with a shuffle as though leaning on a walking stick.

The following day Judy discovered her scissors were missing, and her next door neighbour was greatly puzzled to find a pile of hair cuttings sitting in the middle of her dining room table. Together they made a thorough search of both houses and discovered the scissors upstairs in the neighbour's jewellery box.

This was the only strange thing ever to happen in that house, but it left Judy, Darren and their neighbour totally bemused and wondering to this day whose hair it was.....?

A Disembodied Hand

Meanwhile in a house opposite, Mrs Marilyn Allen and her family have also experienced ghostly "goings on" in their home, built at the same time as Judy's. When they first saw the house they knew it was for them. "It is like being cuddled when you come in here, there is a wonderful warm feeling and we love it," Marilyn said.

Whatever shares the house with them is not malevolent, although it once gave her son Davis, then eight, the fright of his life. Marilyn is often aware of a man's presence in the house, usually upstairs, and his figure has been seen on the landing and stairs.

The first time it appeared, Marilyn was sitting in the lounge watching television with Davis, when a man's hand materialised on the stair rail. A white shape at least six feet tall walked across the hall into the kitchen wall and vanished. Marilyn could actually see the front door through the figure.

She looked at Davis who was just staring after it and asked him what he had seen. "It was a white man. But why could I see through him, Mummy?" he replied, puzzled.

Just after Christmas 1991, when the decorations were still up, Davis went to get ready for bed. Suddenly he came flying downstairs, jumping onto Marilyn's lap in his panic. "He couldn't speak. He was petrified and shaking, and I realised he had encountered something up there."

Between sobs, the youngster said he had been looking for his pyjamas when he had seen a disembodied hand and arm floating towards him. It was a man's right hand wearing an old-fashioned watch with a brown leather strap on the wrist. Davis refused to go upstairs by himself for weeks after this. Now sometimes, early in the morning, Marilyn hears an unknown voice calling out "Davis".

Her elder son, Curtis, refuses to move out of his bedroom into a larger room, because he feels someone is always there with him ......and he likes the company.

THE GHOST WORE A TEE-SHIRT

In the adjoining house, Megan and Malcolm Scambell keep losing things. Little things, keys, earrings - and especially clothes. A drawer full of Megan's tee-shirts completely vanished for several weeks. "We turned the house upside down. We searched everywhere and then one day they were back. I couldn't believe it," Megan said.

Her family has lived at the house since it was built in the early 1980s, and her mother, Dilys Ennion, who has since moved to London, recalls that from the time they moved in things started to disappear. A nurse's silver belt buckle was gone for weeks; keys would vanish from their pegs. No-one saw the things move, but move they did.

Whatever shares their home has never materialised. It simply borrows things.

"You can put something down one minute, turn round and it will have gone. It can be annoying but we are used to it now and whatever has disappeared will always turn up again - eventually," added Malcolm.

A SHY SPIRIT

When Mark Grabham went with his parents to view the council's show house at Mary Rose Avenue, they all knew it was the one for them, and when they moved in a few weeks later it immediately felt like home. Even George, their resident ghost, turned out to welcome them.

On their second day there, Mark, now of Winston Road, Newport, saw the ghostly figure standing at the top of the stairs. "I never felt frightened of him. He was almost like a guardian spirit," said Mark.

The following June, he lost his car keys, lighter and tobacco tin. He hunted everywhere, only to find them some weeks later in the pocket of a winter trench-coat he had not worn for months. "I was certain this was George trying to attract my attention."

Then the ghost started to appear about the house. He wore a black jacket and hat and carried a walking cane. An elderly ghost in his mid-sixties,

George was quite spry, and enjoyed pop music, especially rock and roll.

"Often when I was up in my room listening to the radio or record player, the door would open and I could sense him in there with me. I never really got a good look at his face. He seemed shy and faded in and out whenever I looked."

All the family, including the dog, saw and heard George - even Mark's wife, Tracy, chatted to him one day thinking it was her husband who had just walked upstairs and into the bedroom. It wasn't.

PHANTOMS FROM THE BLITZ

The answer to the unusual level of ghostly activity in such a new housing development may lie beneath the homes. Some of the ground there is very wet and the nearby lake is fed by underground streams. Tons of hardcore and rubble were laid down before the houses could be built - the land at one point was so marshy that a tractor sank.

During the last war almost 5,000 houses in Cowes and East Cowes were destroyed and damaged. In just one air raid on May 5, 1942, a total of 70 men, women and children were killed in the two towns; 80 were seriously injured.

Local councillor, Barry Abraham of Kite Hill Farm, Wootton, confirmed that rubble from those devastated houses was dumped and lay forgotten at an old brickyard in Whippingham, until it was finally used under the foundations of those first houses in Mary Rose Avenue.

Are all the hauntings there related; connected in some strange way with those tragic deaths more than 50 years ago?

Marilyn believes they may well be...especially if one of those men killed in the bombing was wearing an old-fashioned round-faced watch with a brown leather strap.

GHOST IN A PARTY DRESS

An apparition in a brown cloak and a little ghost-child in a party dress made an unwelcome appearance in a newly-built house in Seaview. Nigel Simpkin awoke one night to feel a strange build up of pressure in the room and then a little girl, aged about seven or eight, wearing an ankle-length white party dress came skipping towards the bed. Before she had taken more than a few steps, a brown-cloaked woman walked quickly towards the shimmering child and both suddenly disappeared.

"There was an incredible build up of pressure. It was as if the room was positively charged," Nigel said. "I am also convinced that the pair were mother and daughter."

Nigel, his wife Mary and their four children moved into their new house on the site of a former bungalow in Bullen Road just after Christmas 1989, but they soon realised the atmosphere there was not quite right.

One evening, as Nigel and his daughter Georgina were tiling the bathroom, they heard a stair creak and glimpsed a figure in a long brown hooded robe gliding up the stairs into the airing cupboard. Eight months later, Nigel saw the same figure moving noislessly across the bedroom after emerging from the same cupboard.

Mary saw neither ghost, but always felt she was not alone in the house. A local medium advised the family to move out. The new house was not right for them, she said. But in the meantime she told Mary to place a crucifix in the room, a bulb of garlic in each corner of the kitchen, and to leave bowls of salt and water there. Although dubious about this, Mary followed her instructions....and they worked. The house felt fine again; free from whatever had been troubling it.

Nigel and Mary attempted to trace the history of the site but have so far drawn a blank. They unearthed pieces of old clay churchwarden's pipes in the garden and believe a much older house may once have stood there.

The owner of the former bungalow never experienced any problems in more than 20 years and dismissed the Simpkins' sightings. However at nearby Bullen Cross there once stood a gibbet where bodies were hung and left to rot. Could this have anything to do with the restless spirits? Nigel keeps an open mind.

THE HAUNTED NEWLY-WEDS

It was when their local GP refused to set foot in their flat because it had a ghost that a young East Cowes couple realised they had a problem.

Newly-weds David and Jennifer Godfrey had managed to rent a ground floor flat in a rambling red brick Victorian villa in York Avenue as their first home, back in 1967. Now living in Lake, the Godfreys recall paying rent of three guineas a week for their old flat.

"It was a nice place and we liked it. Originally built for one of Queen Victoria's ladies-in-waiting, it was a very grand house with basement and cellars, high ceilings and huge ten-foot-square windows," said Jennifer.

The first intimation there was something wrong came when David was in the flat by himself a few weeks before the wedding. At 4am he was woken by a thunderous knocking on the front door. When he reached the door he could even feel the vibrations from the heavy cast iron knocker. But as he threw it open, the noise stopped abruptly.

There was no-one there. The front porch was empty and there was no sign of anyone in the grounds. Puzzled, David hunted around thinking someone must have been playing a trick, but found no string tied to the knocker.

Some months later, Jennifer, now married, woke one night to see a figure moving at the bottom of the bed. She called out, thinking it was David - but he was watching television in the next room. As the figure had been wearing a long grey hooded cape, Jennifer could not tell whether it was male or female, but saw it nod its head slightly as if acknowledging her.

David also saw the figure floating past the bed one morning at 4am. As he watched in amazement, it glided over the end of the bed and out of the window.

"I was terrified. I just ducked down under the covers until it had gone," he admitted.

Shortly after that, a neighbour from upstairs knocked at their door in a terrible state one morning. "He just stood there pointing, too shocked to speak. He was as white as a sheet and babbled that he had just seen a ghost. We got him inside and sat him down, and he told us a woman in a grey cloak had floated out through our bedroom window and disappeared into the ground by the basement," David said.

It seems that other people in East Cowes knew of Newport Villa's strange reputation, for when the Godfreys signed on with a local GP he warned them not to expect him to make any home visits there. True to his word, he never did. Newport Villa was demolished in 1988 and the site now stands neglected and overgrown, waiting for a new housing development. But what has become of that hooded grey lady. Does she continue to glide through a non-existent window? And if new flats are built, will there perhaps be an extra, unwanted tenant?

Newport Villa, in once fashionable York Avenue at East Cowes, where a Grey Lady frightened newly-weds David and Jennifer Godfrey.

CHAPTER THIRTEEN

PHANTOM SHIPS AND GHOSTS AT SEA

BOULDNOR'S GHOSTLY GALLEON

A ghostly galleon under full sail was seen one summer night by a couple fishing at Bouldnor, near Yarmouth. Julie Matthews and husband Geoff, could hardly believe their eyes when the vessel came so close inshore that they felt they could almost touch it.

They now run a sub-post office in Ryde, and Julie, a local magistrate, often has to listen to some far-fetched stories when sitting in court. "This was so strange I can still hardly believe it happened to us," she said. "We had a fire on the beach, it was a lovely clear night, and the fish were biting well when we noticed an old three-masted ship like the Mary Rose, out at sea. There were flickering lanterns on the masts and at the bow and stern."

As they watched in amazement, the vessel sailed closer and closer to shore right in front of them - then slowly disappeared. As dawn broke they knew it was no real ship they had seen but an image from the past. Nothing that size could have sailed so close to the shore and not run aground.

This sighting happened in the summer of 1978, some years before the blackened timbers of a mystery vessel were found by divers in the Solent between Yarmouth and Hamstead. It has now been identified as the wreck of a sixteenth century Spanish or Portugese carrack, the Santa Lucia, which ran aground 'athwart Yarmouth' after she was crippled in bad weather close to the shore.

So close in fact, according to Dr David Tomalin - county archaeologist, that her three masts would have been visible even at high tide, until the vessel, which probably resembled Christopher Columbus's flagship the Santa Maria, eventually broke up.

Five centuries later her remains lie entombed in the mud and sand of the Solent. But why did she materialise that night to give Julie and Geoff their incredible glimpse into the past?

THE DOOMED EURYDICE

Have others witnessed such events? The answer is yes. Ghost ships do still sail the treacherous waters off the Isle of Wight. One classic example is HMS Eurydice which capsized and sank in Sandown Bay in March 1878, during a sudden blizzard. Of the 366 men and boys aboard that afternoon, just two were saved.

HMS Eurydice, a 26-gun frigate, was returning to Portsmouth after a tour of Bermuda and the West Indies when disaster struck. Although later raised from Dunnose Point and beached on Bembridge Ledge, she was never re-commissioned. Her bell now hangs in St Paul's Church at Shanklin.

The sinking was witnessed by the young Winston Churchill who was visiting Ventnor with his nurse. The four-year-old boy was watching from the cliffs when Eurydice capsized and a few days later he recalled seeing boats towing ashore bodies recovered from the wreck.

The ghost of James Turner, a twenty-four-year-old marine who went down with the ship, later appeared at his sister's house, where it stood at her bedroom door with water dripping from its wet clothing.

Soon after the tragedy, fishermen and locals began to whisper of a three-masted ship which would disappear if it was approached. Such tales went on for years, but in 1930, Commander F.Lipscombe, a submarine captain, ordered his crew to take evasive action to avoid a three-masted, full-rigged sailing ship - which simply vanished as they watched. Commander Lipscombe was so intrigued by the incident that he later visited the Island, only to be told that he had seen the ghost of the doomed Eurydice.

PHANTOM WRECKS

Further round the coast lurks the notorious Atherfield Ledge, which for centuries, has claimed countless ships and hundreds of lives. These treacherous rocks, just half a mile square, occupy a deadly position in the bay and an extraordinary number of vessels have gone down in this ships' graveyard.

Their ghosts are sometimes still seen, sailing again and again to their doom, and fishermen tell strange tales of hauntings on those lonely beaches...A century ago, Islanders living along that stretch of coast swore that on certain nights they saw a phantom Revenue ship pass by.

More recently, one starlit summer's night as schoolteacher Robin Ford and several friends were enjoying a barbecue, they noticed a three-masted sailing ship drifting ashore in nearby Compton Bay. Outlined by lanterns, the old vessel kept heading towards the beach. When it was just a few yards from shore the lights began to go out and the ship went down, bow-first.

GHOST SHIP ASHORE!

Mrs Joyce Laker saw a ghost ship gliding in one afternoon as she sat in her cottage at Atherfield, where coastguards once lived and kept a look-out.

With her daughter, Niki Ridley, she watched the old ship with sails billowing, being driven ashore; they could even hear people shouting in alarm. The scene was so real that a worried Mrs Laker rang Solent Coastguards to report an emergency! When they arrived however, the emergency service could find no trace of the foundering ship.

That cottage was itself haunted by the ghost of a young coastguard, who would rush down the stairs and out through the front door - whether it was open or closed. The family often heard footsteps overhead, then a young man of about twenty, wearing a sleeveless Fastnet jumper over his shirt and trousers, would dash past them on the stairs, and out. He was quite thin but always went by so quickly he was difficult to see, Niki recalled. "Many of our neighbours had odd things happen to them, too. Atherfield is a very strange place."

AN AURA OF SADNESS AND LONGING

Locals said the ghost had been on his way to help dead and wounded servicemen at a nearby Army billet on the Military Road, which suffered a direct hit in the early hours of April 17, 1942. A German bomber dropped a flare above Brighstone's pre-war holiday camp and followed this up with three bombs which demolished Sea Breeze, an old wooden hotel used as an officers' billet. Ten men were killed that night, and their spirits do not rest easy.

Some thirty years later, Barney's Roadhouse was built on the derelict site of the old hotel and Mrs Julie Clifton of Brook, who ran the pub and nightspot for seven years until 1992, confirms it is haunted. Now manager of the Earl Mountbatten Hospice Shop in Newport, Julie had heard stories about the ghosts at Barney's from regular customers, but always dismissed them as nonsense - until that Thursday morning when she was alone in the cellar and a phantom hand stroked her face.

She had been standing in the middle of the cellar with no curtains or cobwebs anywhere. "It was a cold wisp of cloudy substance and it brushed slowly past my cheek. It stroked me as if it just wanted to touch my skin," said Julie. "There was a feeling of sadness and longing in the air."

After that, she never again dismissed claims by customers and staff that they too had seen or felt a ghost at the roadside pub, usually at the nightclub end of the building.

Ten men were killed here in 1942 and their spirits are not at rest.
Barney's Roadhouse has since been built on the site of Sea Breeze, this old wooden hotel on the Military Road.

THEY WALK THE BEACHES.......

By day the beaches of Compton, Brook and Atherfield are the haunt of sun worshippers through the long summer days, but as the sun goes down and shadows lengthen, those same beaches take on a darker and far more sinister aspect.

The 'Back of the Wight' was once the den of smugglers, wreckers and cut-throats. There is scarcely a cove or chine where tubs of contraband have not come secretly ashore in the dead of night.

Is it the spectre of a long-dead smuggler or a shipwrecked sailor which walks the lonely beaches between Blackgang, Atherfield and Chale? There are some local anglers who will not fish alone there at night. They have seen and heard strange things and talk with reluctance of their experiences.

Peter Shortman of Newington House, Whitwell, has fished from those beaches for years, but one night he caught more than he bargained for. "I was in a little cove on my own near Atherfield Point. There was no-one else there when a man came round the point. He was dressed in a long black jacket and old sailor's cap, and he had boots and seaman's socks on."

By the light of his Tilley lamp, Peter could make out the seaman's features. He was in his fifties and had a beard. "As he went past I said, 'How do'.

"He just looked at me and nodded. I could hear the crunch of his footsteps as he walked off across the stony beach. Then it dawned on me that the tide was in and he could not have come round the point. He had walked out of the sea, but his feet were dry......"

The One That Got Away

A figure in black has also been sighted there by another lone fisherman standing at the water's edge. The angler both saw and heard someone running towards him. The figure was dressed in black and as it closed on him it seemed to fade, although the running steps grew louder.

As it passed, there was what he describes as " the stench of death", and as he stared after sound of the receding steps, the figure appeared once more before it vanished.

Chris Cade, of Gurnard, often spends summer nights fishing at Atherfield, but rarely goes there alone any more.

"One night I was down on the beach and the fish were biting nicely. There was a moon and apart from the crashing of the waves everything was very still. I heard footsteps coming towards me through the shingle. I shone my torch - but the beach was deserted. The footsteps kept on coming. Someone or something was shuffling towards me out of the darkness."

Chris suddenly felt very frightened and reached down to grab a large stone as a weapon. Still the footsteps kept coming and as they passed, his nerve broke. He reeled in, grabbed some of his tackle, and with his lamp pointing towards the sound went in search of fellow-angler Dick Hall.

Dick, of St Mary's Road, Cowes, was taking part in the same competition that April night in 1983, and when he heard Chris's story, he understood his terror. He, too, had experienced something very strange one night while fishing alone at Chale Bay.

"It could have been between one and two o'clock when I sensed I was not alone. I knew there was something standing behind me, although the beach was still empty." Addressing thin air, Dick told it, "I don't know who you are, old mate, but you are making me nervous. I've no wish to bother you so I hope you don't mean me any harm." At that, the unseen presence moved off down the beach towards Chale.

Neville Wheeler was fishing at a spot called 'Coastguards' one night when someone walked through the shingle towards him and placed a hand on his right shoulder. "All right, pal," said Neville, as he looked back to see who was behind. He was alone.

Roger Lawrence, long-time chairman of the Western Wight Angling Club was night fishing at Blackgang, some distance from his friends, when he heard footsteps in the shingle which stopped by his side.

Without looking up, Roger asked, "Anything doing down there?" There was no reply. Roger, who is convinced to this day it was not his imagination, was so unnerved by the incident that he left his tackle and would not return for it until someone went with him.

Atherfield Beach where ghostly footsteps have beeen heard.

CHAPTER FOURTEEN

THE GHOSTS LIVE ON AT VENTNOR

THE HAUNTED OPERATING THEATRE

For almost a century the Royal National Hospital at Ventnor was at the forefront of the fight against the highly infectious disease, tuberculosis.

More than 100,000 patients were treated there. Many were cured. Others weren't so fortunate. Much pioneering and experimental surgery was carried out in the operating theatre, but until the discovery of new and effective drugs, consumption was a highly infectious killer disease.

When the last patient left in May 1964, the hospital doors were ceremonially locked. Five years later, the eleven blocks of balconied cottages which stretched for almost half-a-mile, were demolished, and like a phoenix from the ashes, the Ventnor Botanic Gardens rose from the ruins.

But the old hospital did not give in gracefully. Its death throes brought ghost hunters and psychic investigators from all over the world. The hospital was haunted.

Psychic activity was centred very strongly around the old operating theatre. Virtually the last part of the building to be torn down, it resisted all efforts at demolition by mechanical means. Four tractors, excavators and a ball crane were wrecked in the attempt. The operating theatre was left standing while the rest of the hospital was reduced to rubble.

Mr Roy Dore, of St Lawrence, was curator at the time of the demolition in 1969, and worked for the former Ventnor Urban District Council which bought the 33-acre site from the Ministry of Health.

He recalls what a headache the operating theatre caused for Gosport demolition contractors, Treloar and Sons. "They tried to knock it down with a crane and ball, but the steel cable snapped. Then they brought in a large tracked tractor. Three huge pieces of masonry fell on it, crushing the cab, smashing the transmission and breaking the steel tracks.

"A small caterpillar tractor with a steel hawser was used to pull the walls down, but the hook and cable attachment on the back snapped right off. Another caterpillar tractor became entangled with the broken cable from the first attempt and at that point they gave up."

Long after the rest of the hospital was just a pile of bricks, the empty operating theatre held out. Ether could still be smelled and Roy was among those who noticed it. Workmen talked openly of ghosts. Two men told to demolish the operating theatre with sledgehammers, were confronted by a ghostly figure standing in a doorway.

Moaning, Weeping and Groaning

A young ghost girl looking very pale and ill, with deep sunken eyes, often appeared to keep watch on workmen as they dismantled the old hospital. John Slade of Cowes, remembers her well.

Then a lad of 16, he was doing demolition and salvage work at the site. It was a job he will never forget. Workmen do not frighten easily but those

Once a world renowned chest hospital, the old Royal National Hospital at
Ventnor was demolished to make way for the Botanic Gardens. Ghosts walk here
still, especially at the site of the operating theatre, pictured here between blocks
five and six.

men at Ventnor Hospital always left the site well before darkness fell.
Nearby residents complained constantly - not about the noise and dust from
the demolition, but about the moaning, weeping and groaning coming from
the empty hospital building at night.

Grey misty shapes were seen flitting about the ruins like wisps of cloud,
and the temperature around the old operating theatre always felt several
degrees colder. After the theatre had defied all efforts at demolition by
mechanical means, John was one of those sent in with sledgehammers to
finish the job by hand. "I always felt there was something very wrong there.
It was as if we were being watched all the time. You could be running with
sweat but still feel icy cold. It was a bad place and even after it was pulled
down and levelled, nothing would grow there, no weeds, no grass, and it
still felt cold.

"That operating theatre was the coldest place I have ever worked in. It
was also the hardest to knock down. I don't know why, because it was built
the same as the rest. It just didn't seem to want to go."

John often saw the ghost girl standing in the corner of a ward adjoining
the theatre. She was about ten years old and four feet tall. Her face and
features were solid, the rest of her misty. She would appear in the early
mornings or late afternoons and stand there in the ruined, roofless building,
staring at the workmen. Then she would vanish.

Ghost Hunters Arrive

At last the site was levelled and a car park built on top. But weird things continued to happen. A council surveyor peering through his theodolite saw the ghosts of two Victorian nurses pass in front of the instrument.

The former hospital became a magnet for ghost hunters and students of the supernatural who came from all over the world to try to discover its secret. News of the hauntings even reached American comedian Dick Van Dyke, who was so intrigued by the stories that he had several lengthy transatlantic telephone talks with Roy Dore about the happenings there, and featured them on his popular TV talk-show in the States.

Despite a service of exorcism by local clergy, ghosts continued to make their presence felt. A four-inch thick, armour-plated power cable buried in a trench running across the operating theatre site suddenly stopped functioning, cutting off power to the Garden Tavern. When the trench was opened up, electricity board workers found the thick cable had been neatly chopped into 2ft 6in lengths. How it was done and by whom was never discovered. Meanwhile, one of the engineers replacing the cable suffered a nasty shock - but not from any electrical source.

While using the nearby toilets, converted from the hospital shop, he glanced up to see a ghost sitting on top of the toilet door, watching him. "He came flying out of there with his trousers undone, jumped into his van and left. He never came back," recalled Roy with a grin.

With the car park surfaced over, few visitors now realise there was ever a hospital on the site. But the operating theatre still exerts a malign and disturbing influence. Some dogs grow agitated refusing to walk across that area of the car park, and there is an unusually high number of accidents there.

"If a kiddie falls down and cuts a knee, or someone trips and sprains an ankle, it will always be in that area," said Roy. "It's quite uncanny."

MILLY MEETS A GHOST

From the moment Milly Pugsley saw the old RNH, she loved the place. As a student nurse she spent two happy years there, despite several encounters with the hospital's ghosts. Now a retired nurse tutor, Milly lives at Pan Close, Newport, with a collection of elderly cats whom she claims moved in when she wasn't looking.

When she started her training in September 1952, Milly knew nothing of the hospital's dark reputation, but was introduced to one of the mischievous spirits on the top floor during her very first spell of night duty.

"It was my job to set out the cups and saucers on a tray for the patients' early morning tea. Having done that, I went downstairs to sit in the kitchen with the other nurses. Suddenly there was a loud rattling noise as if someone was moving all the china about. I asked if it was mice. I was told, 'No, it's only the ghost.' This happened every night. We just accepted it and replaced all the cups and saucers before the tea round."

While on night duty in another ward, Milly was allowed two hours sleep and given a bed in the anaesthetic room adjoining the operating theatre. "I was warned to watch out for the ghost there, so taking no chances I always made sure Orlando, a huge ginger tomcat belonging to one of the doctors, came along with me. I figured that if there were any ghosts around, Orlando would see them first," laughed Milly.

Other nurses had told her the ghost liked to pull the bedclothes up around the neck of anyone sleeping in that room, so she never got into bed, just lay on top with Orlando purring beside her.

One night Milly woke suddenly with a feeling that something was wrong. The room was absolutely silent - all the usual hospital noises were missing. "Orlando was standing at the the end of the bed, his fur on end, staring into the corner of the room. This was normally well lit but now was in shadow. There was a blackness there which seemed to be trying to materialise, but I didn't wait to see any more. I was very frightened. The feeling of menace was awful."

Gathering her shoes, cap and the cat, Milly burst out of the room and ran along the verandah to the office. The sister on duty took one look at the terrified girl and said,"I know what's happened to you, my dear. I'll get you a nice cup of tea."

After this experience, Milly heard that the shadow had been seen by other staff, and was said to be the ghost of an anaesthetist in a theatre gown who committed suicide after killing a patient by mistake.

Other incidents happened in wards near the operating theatre. Bells would summon nurses to empty rooms, and on one occasion a ghostly hand set off a patient's alarm when he was unable to breathe, bringing help just in time.

HAND ON THE BEDCLOTHES

Whatever walked those hospital wards was also seen by patients. During 1957, Mrs Violet Newman of London, was treated at Ventnor and actually encountered one of its ghosts.

One night as she lay in her bed facing the verandah, Violet saw the french doors swing open and a girl step into the room. Thinking it was a fellow patient she called out a greeting. Then, suddenly, one of the hospital cats which was in the room with her, rushed off down the corridor, its tail and fur standing on end. And when Violet glanced back, she was alone. The girl had disappeared.

On another occasion, she was woken from a deep sleep to feel her bedclothes being rolled down, although the room was empty. It was the nights that were the worst time." Strange things could happen then," said Violet.

AND STILL IT GOES ON.....

Simon Goodenough doesn't believe in ghosts. A sceptic of the supernatural, he was sure the tales of hauntings at the old hospital were just ridiculous ..... until he met the ghost of a long-dead patient.

With a scientific background and 12 years at Kew Gardens behind him, Simon took over as curator of the Ventnor Botanic Gardens in 1985. With

Deb, his wife, who is also an expert in horticulture, and a staff of gardeners and workmen, Simon has transformed the former hospital gardens into a renowned centre of botanic excellence. It is informally twinned with gardens in New Zealand which, curiously, are also in the grounds of an old tuberculosis hospital.

After just two weeks at Ventnor, Simon and Deb began to experience things they couldn't explain - silly little things - but puzzling all the same. The couple went into the new temperate house to check their plants and found both doors locked behind them - although the only set of keys was in Simon's pocket.

The open hospital wards where patients enjoyed the bracing sea air, winter and summer, have been converted into potting sheds. Here, seeds, cuttings, young plants and the the gardens' index file system are kept. On several mornings, Simon has arrived to find that the index cards have been removed from their files, neatly sorted, and stacked into piles on the potting bench. The doors are always still locked and padlocked. There is no sign of a break-in, just neat little piles of white cards sorted by a hand that is no longer living.

"Whatever is there seems curious about our work. The feeling we get is benign. It seems to approve of what we are doing," said Simon.

A Sickly Ghost

For several years now, in the week before Christmas, Simon and Deb have been intrigued by the strong tantalising smell of hot cinnamon punch wafting around them as they work in the potting shed. "We have both noticed it but can never find out where it is coming from," said Simon.

The mystery was solved after a chance remark to Dr Eric Laidlaw, once a doctor at the old RNH. He remembered it was a hospital tradition to serve hot punch at Christmas. Huge steaming bowls would be taken round on a trolley to all the patients - including those in the open wards.

That kindly potting shed ghost may even have saved Deb's life on the night of the great hurricane in October 1987. As she worked there alone, unaware of the impending storm, she felt an overwhelming urge to get out. It was as if someone was telling her to drop everything and leave immediately. Deb was so unnerved that she obeyed her premonition and went home.

Later that night, the potting shed was crushed when a huge tree fell right on top of it. Surveying the damage next morning, Deb said a heartfelt thanks to whoever had tried to warn her.

One evening soon after he started his new job, Simon met a patient from the old hospital near the potting shed. "We chatted a while. He asked if I been there long. I replied about three months."

The man in his forties who appeared very drawn and pale, told Simon, "I have been in the hospital now for six months." He then said 'cheerio', and wandered off.

"What he had said suddenly hit me and as I drove out of the car park all the hairs on the back of my neck stood on end. I had just seen a ghost." Then Simon's natural scepticism took over. He told himself the man had come from a nursing home nearby. However, he saw the same figure two years later. This time the apparition did not speak but vanished as Simon watched. It wore the same clothes as before, a heavy, old-fashioned, Edwardian flannel suit, and still looked very ill.

"I was sure then that I had been speaking to a ghost... a very sickly and consumptive one who must have died here at Ventnor."

The potting shed where a ghost with consumption still walks.

CHAPTER FIFTEEN

KNIGHTON GORGES....THE ISLAND'S MOST HAUNTED HOUSE

It has been called the most haunted place on the Island, and even today the long-vanished house of Knighton Gorges seems determined to live up to its reputation. Strange things happen there still, and according to some people, what was once described as the most beautiful of the Island's ancient manors, can still be seen at certain times of the year. (The haunted history of the house is told in Ghosts of the Isle of Wight).

Since he was a boy, Knighton Gorges has held a strange fascination for Ivor Davies, a retired consultant engineer and former Mayor of South Wight Borough Council. Ivor fulfilled a childhood dream when he bought six acres of land on which the old house once stood, where he is converting a 17th century stone barn into a home for himself and family.

Ivor has spent years researching the history of Knighton Gorges, and although he has never seen or heard a ghost there, he is quite prepared to believe that others have. "I go there every day and I would love to see something. So many people have told me of their experiences that I am quite disappointed nothing has yet happened for me," said Ivor, who recalls cycling out to Knighton Gorges as a boy to play there with friends.

"It was always my dream to live there, and it looks as though I shall soon be able to give Knighton Gorges as my address. People are drawn to the place but I understand the strange attraction that brings them. I am not a speculator. I am not going to develop Knighton Gorges in any way."

With the help of old documents, records and engravings, Ivor has been able to trace the outlines of the old house. He has found the remains of the foundations and part of the gardens but has not undertaken any excavations himself for fear of disturbing important archaeological evidence. Ivor is patiently waiting for the county archaeological officer to organise a proper "dig" there one day. He has traced the house's owners back to the Middle Ages and has his own ideas on its sudden demolition. Local legend tells that it was done out of spite by Captain Maurice George Bisset when his eldest daughter married against his wishes. The bitter old man died, it was said, in a tiny gardener's cottage in the grounds, breathing his last as the timbers and stones crashed down.

Ivor holds a less romantic but far more practical theory. His researches have shown that Captain Bisset died at his Scottish estate, Lessendrum, on December 16, 1821. Ivor thinks the upkeep of the old house was simply too great. It had fallen into disrepair and was costing too much to maintain. "I believe Captain Bisset had it demolished and sold off everything he could."

Evidence to support this theory survives just a few miles away. The back staircase from Knighton Gorges, once used by servants, is now in Horringford House, Arreton, while part of the newer main staircase is at nearby Langbridge House, Newchurch. Stone and timber from the old manor is said to have been used in several Island houses built in the 1820s. So the old house at Knighton Gorges lives on......

The Island's most haunted place - all that remains of the most beautiful of the Island's ancient manors is a kitchen wall hidden amongst the pines.

Two staircases survived the demolition. One, pictured left, complete with ghost, was installed in Langbridge House, Newchurch; the other is at Horringford House, near Haseley.

A GHOST ON THE STAIRS

The gleaming, polished wooden staircase which once graced the splendid hall in Knighton Gorges is ending its days less than a mile from the long-gone manor house. Local nobility and distinguished visitors such as John Wilkes, David Garrick and Sir Joshua Reynolds once walked its boards.

Now the staircase, or at least part of it, has been incorporated into nearby Langbridge House, Newchurch - along with one of the manor's ancient ghosts. The bent and hooded figure of an elderly friar was seen by former Newchurch resident, Mrs Ivy Welstead, during a meeting of the local Women's Institute at the old house.

Ivy recalled: "He was aged about seventy, not solid but transparent and rather grey. He looked a very benevolent old gentleman and I was not at all frightened. He was standing at the top of the staircase, and then just disappeared into a wall."

Ivy decided to keep this to herself for she thought some of her fellow WI members might be alarmed, but she later told Mrs Jill Salmon and her husband Frank, owners of Langbridge since 1968, of her experience. Neither Frank, a former airline pilot, nor ex-air stewardess Jill, has ever seen their ghost, and apart from one or two odd accidents on the staircase they have always been happy there.

Did the grey friar accompany the old staircase to Langbridge House? It seems likely, for a former owner, Parson James Tooke, purchased an assortment of materials from Knighton Gorges after it was demolished. Distinctively carved doors and door frames, beams, tiles and stonework from the old mansion live on in Langbridge House. The Reverend Tooke even built a small chapel on the side of the house, which was later pressed into service as a Sunday School and then a village meeting hall.

Langbridge House, built in 1725 on the site of an earlier farmhouse, stands opposite the Old School House (whose ghostly history is featured elsewhere in this book). Parson Tooke's bargain buys from Knighton Gorges, which was pulled down in 1821, were later incorporated into Langbridge House when it was remodelled. But the vicar got more than he bargained for with the old staircase. Does a weary spirit which once haunted the manor live on in those vestiges of its former glory?

PHANTOM IN A BALL GOWN

Knighton Gorges continues to draw people. Its reputation as the Island's most haunted place is well known, and every New Year's Eve hopeful ghost hunters converge there hoping for a glimpse of the old house which is said to materialise on that night.

Among the watchers on December 31, 1982, was Judy Axford, who went with a friend. With strong psychic abilities, Judy had already experienced something strange at Newchurch a few years earlier. (See Chapter 8). As the two women stood by the old stone gateposts on the drive, Judy became aware of a woman in a long mauve dress moving towards them at speed. "The figure came from the left of the gateposts. It was gliding very quickly but I could not make out its feet or legs. It was a young woman with fair hair piled high on top of her head. She appeared to be wearing a very decorative ball-gown. It was the colour of the gown that first caught my attention. It was absolutely gorgeous," Judy added.

Suddenly she felt icy cold and with her friend, who had also seen the figure, Judy got back into her car and drove off up Knighton Shute before her passenger had even closed her door.

Later that night, they returned to Newchurch and parked outside the 900-year-old church at the top of Newchurch Shute. "We sat there quietly, looking out over the village in the direction of Knighton Gorges, hoping we might see the house, but from a safe distance."

They saw nothing at all. Newchurch slumbered through the old year and into the new. But Judy did hear something....it was the sound of a whip cracking. A ghostly echo, perhaps, from a phantom carriage carrying revellers from that ball where the mauve lady had obviously been a guest.

GHOSTLY GREEN WINDOWS

As midnight approached on New Year's Eve 1991, Brian Perkins, his wife Lois, and two friends, decided to drive out to Knighton Gorges to see if any of the stories about the old house re-appearing on that night were true.

Taking their Doberman bitch, Anya, along with them, they drove out to Knighton where they were amazed to find many others with the same idea. Brian, a crane operator, of Partlands Avenue, Ryde, said it had been a cold clear night with good visibility.

"We walked through the gateposts into the grounds. Just after midnight we saw the outline of a stone window appear in the distance. It was glowing and a luminous green colour."

The apparition lasted for almost a minute and during this time he and the others ran towards it, even climbing a barbed wire fence to get closer. The window faded, re-appeared, and then faded away again. All four agreed it had been a large, square, ground floor stone window. As they returned to the van, Brian heard the sound of a horse and carriage clattering through the gates of Knighton Gorges. He could see nothing but the phantom folds of a blue cloak high above the ground...where a spectral coachman had been sitting.

Meanwhile back in their van, the dog who was usually very quiet, was agitated, refusing to calm down until they had put Knighton Gorges and its haunting atmosphere far behind them.

"We were all astonished by what we had seen. We had not gone expecting anything to happen. It was all supposed to be a bit of a laugh. But I certainly believe there is something there now. I don't know about the others, but I will return again next New Year's Eve for sure," vowed Brian.

BATHED IN AN EERIE LIGHT

One balmy autumn evening back in 1969, Ray Harvey and a girlfriend were sitting in his car in a lay-by just off the Downs road, listening to the radio and looking out over Sandown Bay. The evening was dark and still.

Suddenly, the countryside grew as bright as day and for a very short time, perhaps two or three seconds, daylight appeared over Knighton Gorges.

"There was no sound, it was no lightning flash, simply a brief period of daylight in what had been a lovely dark September night. It was like an eclipse in reverse. We both saw it, but to this day, I have absolutely no idea what it was," said Ray.

He was amazed to find nothing on the local news to explain the strange event, and more surprised that no-one else had seen it. "For those brief moments everything in the area of Knighton Gorges was bathed in light."

Was it perhaps the old house making one of its rare appearances? From where he was sitting, Ray couldn't see.

Although she was not the girlfriend involved, Ray's wife Mandy certainly doesn't scoff at this tale, for she too has seen something strange and disturbing at Knighton Gorges.

RIDDLE OF THE STONE CREATURES

Mandy, a former nurse, is one of the few who have seen the stone lions atop the old gateposts at Knighton Gorges. As a teenager she frequently passed the pillars while out horseriding and was attracted to the beasts, which she described as "large crouching lions with their paws in front, carved out of old weathered grey stone."

Years later, while working in Newchurch, Mandy drove past the old gateposts regularly. One day she noticed the stone beasts were gone but when she asked at work what had happened to them, everyone laughed and told her there had been nothing on those gateposts in living memory.

There are no stone creatures here. This photograph taken in 1949 shows only the gateposts with their 'loaves of bread'.

A REAL MYSTERY TOUR

Countless times in the 1950s and early '60s, local coach driver Ted Perry took visitors on mystery tours down Knighton Shute and through Newchurch. He always stopped by the gateposts to tell his passengers the story of Knighton Gorges; of how the old house had been demolished and only the gateposts, with their heraldic lions on top, had been spared.

Ted has long since retired to grow prize-winning fuschias at his cottage in Brading Mall. It was a letter he wrote to the IW County Press in 1965 that first posed the riddle of the stone creatures which has intrigued Islanders ever since.

Ted had taken his passengers past the gateposts and stopped as usual to tell them the Knighton Gorges story. But to his amazement when he looked at the pillars, the animals had disappeared. Fearing they had been stolen, he dashed off an angry letter to the County Press to ask if anyone knew where they were. For a long while after this, controversy raged.

A number of Islanders claimed to have seen the creatures despite photographs dating from 1916 and 1949 which provided clear evidence that the only ornamentation in recent years had been the circular hoops known locally as 'loaves of bread', a traditional sign to hungry travellers that they would be given bread and water at the kitchen door to speed them on their way.

Ted now accepts the creatures weren't there - although he had been pointing them out to his passengers for years. "None of them ever said a word. They must have thought I was mad...... or seen the figures themselves," he laughed.

WOMAN WITHOUT A FACE

A hooded figure in a grey cloak terrified three nurses late one night, as they drove past the gates to the old house. Dilys Ennion was at the wheel when the women returned from teaching a First Aid class.

"We saw a woman wearing a grey hooded cape, walking alone in the dark. One of my passengers got out to ask if she needed a lift. Suddenly she screamed and came flying back to the car, shrieking at me to drive away."

The agitated nurse told her friends that the woman had no face, just a grey misty emptiness where her features should have been.

Further along Ashey Road the nurses passed a police patrol car. Recognising the officers from their work in the Casualty Department, the women asked them to go and check out the mysterious figure.

"They called at our flat later that night to say they had found nothing. The road was empty. They laughed and told us we had dreamt it. But we all saw her and we know she was a ghost. To this day, I always lock my car doors if I have to drive along that road," said Dilys with a shiver.

CHAPTER SIXTEEN

CONVERSATIONS WITH GHOSTS

Most ghosts are seen but never heard. A few however talk, laugh, shout, whisper and moan, while some even argue....

APPARITIONS WHO ARGUED

Lillie Langtry stayed there, as did Emperor Napoleon III and his Empress Eugenie. Now, Beaulieu House in Queen's Road at Cowes, has visitors of a more ethereal kind...ghosts who argue.

John Wilkinson, who has owned the early Victorian house overlooking the Solent since 1978, has neither seen nor heard his ghostly guests, but Pat who shares his home, has encountered one of them, and his cleaner has confronted others.

"She was a slim woman in her late forties with greying hair pulled back into a bun. It was her exquisite long full skirt in charcoal grey which caught my eye. She also wore a light grey high-necked blouse with leg o'mutton sleeves," Pat recalled.

This rather daunting spinsterish ghost has been seen in the entrance hall, moving between the lounge and dining room - the same part of the house frequented by a more modern looking phantom dressed in the style of the 1940s, which startled John's cleaning lady one morning. Wearing a navy blue skirt and a blue short-sleeved jumper, this ghost came 'scampering' out from the kitchen towards the front door and disappeared into the dining room.

"I followed her straight in there and found the room was completely empty. She had simply vanished into thin air," said the domestic, who is also named Pat. "She was a little round-faced woman in her late fifties, and it was the way she was scurrying, in tiny running steps, that was so odd."

Odder still was the time Pat (the cleaner) heard two ghosts quarrelling, shouting at each other at the tops of their voices, although she could not make out a single word they were saying.

"I had been working on the top floor when I heard voices in the hall," said Pat. "They were yelling and sounded furious. I was really quite frightened because I thought the house was empty. I shouted out, `Who's there?' , but they took no notice. I went down the stairs and called out again. This time the sounds stopped abruptly, as if someone had switched them off."

Then Pat noticed how cold the house had become. It was winter and the central heating was on in every room, but despite the radiators which were still on, the whole house felt icy cold. "It was like the sort of cold you get in a deep freeze. It was uncanny."

Growing more and more alarmed, she checked every room in the house. They were all cold, except for one tiny top-floor room which had once been the nursery and playroom. It was the only warm place in the entire building, and there she remained, listening, in case those voices returned.

John and Pat have no idea who or what their ghosts once were, and since the 150 year old house was renovated, they haven't been heard or seen. Polly the boxer dog sometimes senses a presence moving in the hallway, but which ghost it is, she never lets on......

VOICES FROM THE PAST

A ground floor apartment in a new luxurious development on Cowes seafront, with spectacular Solent views, would seem an unlikely place to find a couple of ghosts. But Mrs Margaret Foster and her husband have heard and felt them there.

A medium all her life, Margaret has always had a special rapport with animals and two beautiful black cats share the apartment. Neither animal was around however, when Margaret started to feel the bedclothes being bunched around her as she lay in bed at night.

"It was as if someone was trying to tuck me in. This went on a couple of times a week for two months. I could feel someone or something moving my duvet, but there was never anyone there. Finally I told whatever was responsible to stop. I did it in a very polite way and I have never had any more trouble after that."

In the next-door bedroom, Mr Foster also had a couple of ghostly visitors. He described how at 2 o'clock one morning, he heard the sound of a door opening and footsteps entering his room. Yet the bedroom door remained firmly shut. Then a voice, a beautifully-spoken cultured voice announced, "Whenever I come into this room, it always feels so cold and damp."Her unseen companion whispered, "Hush, they will hear you."

Intrigued, Mr Foster waited and listened, but he heard no more voices that night , or any night since. It was, he said, impossible for him to have heard people in nearby apartments. "These two ladies were in the room with me... or at least in a room of the old house which once stood on this site."

The rambling late-Victorian house which was demolished in the 1980's, was once the home of an elderly lady and her young companion. The Fosters believe what they heard and felt may have been faint echoes from the old houses's past in their otherwise modern, warm and comfortable home.

THE GHOST'S WARNING

Betty Haunt Lane, as the name suggests, has a reputation for being haunted. As the mist rolls across Alvington Valley, strange things can happen there. At one end of the lane which winds between the Newport-Calbourne Road and Forest Road, the shade of 'Buxom Betty', the smuggler's daughter who met a bad end two centuries ago, is said to walk.

Betty fell in love with an Excise officer and betrayed her comrades who were hiding their contraband at the nearby Blacksmiths Arms Inn. Most were captured, but a few escaped. They came back for Betty. Her death was slow and painful, and it is said that her screams and moans may still be heard on dark moonless nights in Betty Haunt Lane.

At the far end of the lane is the IW Donkey Sanctuary, and it is here that

Charlie Clarke, who runs the charity with his wife Cheryl, received a warning from a ghost. Charlie, a former postman, was working at the sanctuary just off Vittlefields crossroads one summer afternoon in 1988, when Ben, his labrador, started barking furiously. Looking towards the gate, Charlie saw a woman aged about twenty-five standing there.

"She was dressed in poor shabby clothes and looked as if she had just come from a jumble sale. Speaking very slowly in a broad Isle of Wight accent, she told me she lived in a cottage down the lane."

The woman warned Charlie never to go to the sanctuary on a foggy night without Ben. "You must never come here without the dog when the mist comes across," she urged - not once but five times. Promising she would return, the woman wished Charlie "Good-day".

"I said goodbye and turned back to the stables feeling extremely relieved that she had gone. There was something distinctly strange about her. She was very dull-witted, stupid almost, and I had been very uneasy talking to her."

As he walked away from the woman in the old-fashioned attire, Charlie felt his hair stand on end and he went icy cold. Turning back towards the gate, he saw the woman had vanished. He looked up and down the lane for her, even climbing the gate to peer over the hedge, but she was nowhere to be found.

"I had been talking to a ghost and it is something I never want to do again," admitted Charlie. "Despite her promise she has not returned...yet...and I hope she never does."

Charlie lives the other side of Parkhurst Forest and always checks his donkeys late at night. However since his encounter with the ghost he often feels uneasy, as if he is being watched.

And whenever the fog rolls in across the valley as darkness falls, Charlie heeds her warning. He never visits his donkeys...unless he has a dog with him.